Anxiety Transformed is a book we desperately need. Anxiety is on the rise across all generations and alarmingly high among millennials and generation Z. At the same time, we in campus ministry are seeing real spiritual hunger among young people, paired with a skepticism about the Christian church due to public failures and polarization. The Church needs hope in the form of real, practical help with anxiety—and thanks be to God, that hope is rising. Historically Christian insights and prayer disciplines can open us to God's gracious transforming work in our troubled souls. Nader Sahyouni draws from his life experience and from his work in counseling and spiritual direction to deliver relevant insights and practical help for those experiencing anxiety. The book draws from emerging neuroscience as well as spiritual formation and traditional therapy. Nader has practiced all the disciplines he suggests and has helped others practice them as well. May God use them to renew his healing, transforming work in our troubled world.

—Jason Jensen
Vice President, Spiritual Foundations
InterVarsity Christian Fellowship

I have been sensing, of late, a need to pay careful attention to our formation as Christians through trials, through our weaknesses. In *Anxiety Transformed*, Nader Sahyouni has given just such attention to our fears. His book is personal, openly sharing his own experience of anxiety along with many stories of those he has helped. It is informed, drawing from research in psychology and spiritual practice. It is Christian, rooted in Scripture and in the rich traditions of the faith uniquely embodied in Sahyouni's own life. And it is practical, filled with prayer practices and concrete steps toward growth in Christ. I see *Anxiety Transformed* as a helpful resource for the anxious, for those in the helping professions, and for Christians longing to grow deeper in their faith through their own struggles.

Author of *The Brazos I*

D1410498

There are books about cognitive therapy for anxiety, others about exposure therapy for anxiety, books about spiritual direction for anxiety, or about relaxation techniques for anxiety, and there are books about healing trauma that can be the underlying source of anxiety. But other than this book by Nader Sahyouni, I am not aware of any book that talks about *all* these pieces and how they fit together. (Just the section on the recent discoveries regarding memory reconsolidation and how this new information supports trauma-healing work, is worth the price of the book.)

—Karl D. Lehman, M.D.
Board certified psychiatrist with thirty-
five years of clinical experience
Developer of the Immanuel Approach (along with Dr. Jim Wilder)
Author of *Outsmarting Yourself* and
The Immanuel Approach: For Emotional Healing and for Life

Anyone who has experienced anxiety will find the book *Anxiety Transformed* by Nader Sahyouni to be a helpful resource. Filled with many personal life experiences, this book shows a deep understanding of the spiritual and emotional roots of anxiety from both a psychological and biblical perspective. It is filled with exercises that will enable the reader to comprehend the concepts and apply the practical suggestions to their life situation. A practical, balanced, and effective approach.

—Dr. David Sherbino
Professor of Pastoral Ministry and Spiritual
Formation, Tyndale Seminary
Minister, The Presbyterian Church in Canada

Anxiety Transformed is a refreshing and compelling blend of spiritual wisdom from the author's deep and broad experience as a spiritual director and psychological insight based on neuroscience, current research, and his experience as an effective therapist. Nader Sahyouni's accessible and authentic personal stories demonstrate he has lived with these principles and tested them in his own life. His examples from those with whom he has worked also show they work for others as well! *Anxiety*

Transformed tells the reader how to fight smart against unwanted anxiety, leveraging its effects into a deep, meaningful, and joyful connection to God.

—Charlotte E. Tsuyuki Lehman, M.Div.
Pastor, Reba Place Church, Evanston, Illinois

ANXIETY
TRANSFORMED

Prayer that Brings Enduring Change

X. Nader Sahyouni, DMin, LCPC

Crossing Place Media
Skokie, Illinois 60076

Published in Skokie, Illinois, Crossing Place Media

All Scripture quotations, unless otherwise indicated, are taken from the Holy Bible, New International Version®, NIV®. Copyright ©1973, 1978, 1984, 2011 by Biblica, Inc.™ Used by permission of Zondervan. All rights reserved worldwide. www.zondervan.com. The "NIV" and "New International Version" are trademarks registered in the United States Patent and Trademark Office by Biblica, Inc.™

Scripture quotations marked (GNT) are from Good News Translation in Today's English Version- Second Edition Copyright © 1992 by American Bible Society. Used by Permission.

Cover design: Wendy York, Dave Jackson
Cover photos: Upsplash: Nikolas Noonan, Tj Holowaychuk
Book design: Dave Jackson

Printed in the United States of America

For further information visit
MySpiritualDirector.com

To my grandson,
May your generation know peace

CONTENTS

ACKNOWLEDGEMENTS

There are so many people whose wisdom, input, and support helped me to create this book. First, I wish to thank Dave and Neta Jackson for all their coaching and wisdom about the process of writing, and their continual encouragement. I also would like to thank Dr. Karl Lehman, M.D., for all the consultation on the topics in this book and the various aspects of brain science involved. A special thank you to Dennis Anderson for his encouragement regarding Centering Prayer, and to Father Matt Linn, S.J., for inspiring the last chapter in this book. A big thank you goes to all those who gave me permission to share some of their stories. I am grateful for all I have learned from my work at Compass Counseling, at InterVarsity Christian Fellowship's department of Spiritual Foundations, as well as my professors at Tyndale Seminary. Many thanks also to all my friends and family for their prayer and encouragement. A special thanks goes to my wife, Marijean, whose support was unceasing in emotional, spiritual, and administrative ways.

INTRODUCTION

I WAS ABOUT THREE YEARS OLD, sitting on my father's lap, on an airplane high up in the air while he pointed out the clouds and ocean below. But all I could think of was that we were going to fall out of the sky at any moment. I cried in my three-year-old fear, and my father tried to reassure me that everything was fine.

In many ways, this early memory is a good example of what it's like for us in our anxiety with God. We cry to him about something that feels fearful, and he tries to reassure us.

Most of us who follow Christ turn to God in our need—*give us our daily bread, forgive us our sins, heal our diseases and our relationships.* Similarly, when we suffer times of anxiety, many of us also instinctively turn to God. For those with faith in Jesus Christ, it makes sense to turn to him for help in dealing with anxiety. That is what this book is about: turning to God in times of anxiety. Except it's not just about taking that first step in asking God for help, it's about taking the second, third, and fourth steps—eventually leading to life-giving patterns of prayer for those who struggle with anxiety. These new patterns help us develop a healthy spirituality and can help reduce anxiety.

Answers to anxiety are available in Scripture, but for many they don't seem to bring much relief. "Do not be afraid . . ." are words spoken to us in the Scriptures on multiple occasions. We believe the Scriptures, and yet we are anxious. For someone suffering from anxiety, hearing the words, "You just need to have more faith," is rarely helpful. That admonition may well be true, but faith is not something we can work up like a positive thinking exercise. Nonetheless, how faith helps to reduce anxiety, and the role of prayer in that process, is one of the key themes of this book.

I should note, however, that while some of the suggestions in this book may be helpful in addressing one type of anxiety, they may not help with other types. It is beyond the scope of this book to look at all types of anxieties (for example, we don't look at panic disorder). In addition, anxiety unfortunately shows up in other disorders that are not classified as anxiety disorders in the *Diagnostic and Statistical Manual of Mental Disorders* current version (version five). Individuals who suffer from Obsessive Compulsive Disorder (OCD) or Post Traumatic Stress Disorder (PTSD) are good examples of this. These individuals may suffer significant anxiety, but PTSD and OCD are not listed as anxiety disorders. Yet some of the suggestions in this book will hopefully be helpful as adjunct support for those in treatment for PTSD and OCD.

This work is intended to offer help to receive, integrate, and live out what the Scriptures say about prayer and anxiety. It does not—and I can't emphasize this enough—replace the role of counseling or psychotherapy. It most definitely does not replace the need for medication where that's appropriate. Just as I entrust my life into a surgeon's hands during an operation, I also bring the surgery to God in prayer. The same is true with anxiety. Even as we take all the steps that are wise, whether going through a workbook on anxiety, seeing the right therapist, or, if recommended, adding medications from a psychiatrist, we still pray. Our need, our desire, and God's invitation to pray through our struggle with anxiety is still present. This is especially true because anxiety has components that are related to our life of faith.

In my periods of anxiety, I have learned some lessons about how to pray more effectively about anxiety. Exploring which prayer patterns are most helpful in our relationship with God will be one of the major themes explored in this book. I do not claim that I have arrived at complete healing or that I have any silver bullets. Some of the suggestions in this book are difficult and many are for the long term. I do not claim to be able to do them all myself at all times and in all situations. God's grace is given us in different measures at different times. These are not magical cures or recipes for getting rid of anxiety. They are, rather, suggestions for how to cultivate spiritual health in response to anxiety, how to engage with God's grace as it is given to us in seasons of anxiety, and how to embrace hope in the middle of it.

This can lead to an even deeper topic: spiritual formation. God is at work in us as we struggle with anxiety in ways that parallel and support the work of therapy. And we'll explore those parallels. We'll look at what God may be inviting us toward—namely, how it seems God uses our prayer life during anxiety to bring about spiritually formative experiences. We will try to develop an understanding of how we can respond to anxiety in prayer in a way that best facilitates and cooperates with God's desires for our spiritual growth. In doing so we can come to see anxiety as an opportunity for spiritual growth that has eternal value.

For some people who are more naturally drawn to prayer, many of the suggestions in this book will seem exciting and inviting. For others they may seem difficult to relate to. Richard Foster, in his book *Streams of Living Water*, talks about six traditions in the Christian life through which we can hope to imitate Jesus: Contemplative, Holiness, Charismatic, Social Justice, Evangelical, and Incarnational. In this book, I draw most from the contemplative tradition. For those most naturally drawn to and gifted in contemplative practices, this book will be an easy fit. The question then is, if my experience of Jesus is most potently expressed in one of the other five traditions, is the content of this book of value to me? I would argue an emphatic yes. We may not all be called to the many aspects of contemplative prayer, but we are all called to pray and to practice some types of loving contemplation of God. Similarly, we may not all be called to life as evangelists, but we *are* all called to evangelize; we may not be called to living among the poor, yet we *are* all called to give to the poor, and so on. Foster makes this clear at the end of every chapter that describes one of these traditions. Although we may have a particularly strong calling in one of them, we are indeed called to all of them.[1]

In this book, I'll draw on my studies and practice of Spiritual Direction (North Park Theological Seminary), Mental Health Counseling (Northeastern Illinois University), and Spiritual Formation (Tyndale University). To a lesser degree, I will draw on my earlier exposure to neuroscience gained during the research for my first master's degree on brain control of eye movements. This exposure helped me include some of the newer insights from the world of brain science. However, this science continues to develop very quickly, and the complexities involved are well beyond the scope of this book. Insights from that realm of study are current to the best of my understanding, but that field continues to evolve at a rapid pace. Also, while all explanations are as thorough as possible for a book like this, they do not cover all complexities.[2] Many thanks to Dr. Karl Lehman for the consultations that allowed me to pull much of what I was learning together. Finally, I will also bring to bear my own journey of learning to pray through anxiety and difficulty and what I've learned about spiritual formation in the process.

I saw the origins of my history of anxiety firsthand in my own mother, but it came into clearer focus for me in one of my counseling classes. The assignment was to draw a genogram—basically a family tree—and look for family patterns that influence mental health over generations. I became aware that it went back even further than my mother.

I was born in Cairo, Egypt, and grew up in Beirut, Lebanon. My maternal grandmother is from the town of Antioch, mentioned in the book of Acts in the New Testament. She had thirteen children, but only six survived to adulthood. I believe most of her children died in outbreaks of typhus or Spanish flu around the time of World War I. I heard a story of her going into the hospital with three sick children and leaving with none. One of her children, who lived into his early twenties, died from pneumonia. Apparently, that was the straw that broke the camel's back for her mental health; it was just too much for her. You can imagine the levels of loss and anxiety this woman lived with as she lost eight of thirteen children.

I unfortunately never knew her because she died before I was born. I am told that her grief was so heavy she had to leave her children in the care of her sister as she entered a convent, where the nuns cared for her. I imagine they taught her how to pray, because my mother used to tell me stories of my grandmother's prayer life—how she used to shut the door of her bedroom for one or two hours of prayer a day. It wouldn't matter what was going on outside her door, she would not open it. In a blessed sort of way, I feel like I ended up inheriting some of that experience of finding strength, solace, comfort, and healing in spending time with God.

Not surprisingly, my mother grew up with a lot of anxieties in her family around health and illness that carried into her own life. I ended up inheriting a lovely bouquet of anxieties around health myself. My response was not too different from my grandmother's, except that I had the benefit of psychology in addition to spiritual help. I did not go to a convent as she did, but I did look for answers in all the Christian traditions I encountered, as well as in psychology.

I grew up with spiritual input from Orthodox, Catholic, and Protestant perspectives. My father is from an Antiochian Orthodox church denomination that reconciled with Rome in the 1720s. They are called Greek Catholics instead of Roman Catholics. My mother's main spiritual influence was the American Presbyterian mission school she attended in Cairo.

On Sundays when we were kids in Beirut, my siblings and I would attend an evangelical Sunday school, and then we'd walk to the Byzantine liturgy. In addition, I attended a French Catholic school (that's not all that unusual in Lebanon, as most middle-class Christian families send their kids to private French schools).

When I was eleven years old in the spring of 1975, the civil war in Lebanon began. We immigrated to the United States two and a half years later. During my college years in the US, I was involved with InterVarsity Christian Fellowship. Many of the people I met in InterVarsity introduced me to the Vineyard Church, where my attendance opened me to experiences in the charismatic world as well.

Because of all these influences, I tried to learn from the Orthodox, the Catholics, the Charismatics, and the Evangelicals all prayer practices that might help. Hence, this book reflects some of my openness to a variety of Christian traditions. What I have found in terms of prayer is that there are no short-term answers. The practices of prayer that God calls us into in the face of anxiety are for the long run. They help establish a new path that bends away from anxiety and toward a greater spiritual maturity and peace. The insights and practices in this book take time, but they are powerful. Not only can they reduce long-term anxiety, but they can revolutionize our relationship with God. It is a long-term, life-changing, and eternally impacting set of practices.

This book is divided into three parts.

The first part deals with responding to anxious feelings in prayer. I will lay out an integration of theology and psychology to provide a framework for understanding how to respond to anxiety in prayer. The result of this integration is a prayer model that can be used in the face of immediate anxiety.

The second part deals with the roots of the anxious feelings, which often lie in past trauma. My guess is that as you seek God's help in dealing with anxiety, he will lead you to someone, or more than one person, to help you process your root causes. As we do so, there are ways we can pray fruitfully, based on Scripture and psychology, in support of God's healing work in our lives.

The third part is about building up our spiritual immune system so we are less likely to be affected by anxiety, and even when we are affected, the impact becomes less severe. This part focuses on what it means for an anxious person to learn to trust God. How do we trust God in a way that makes a difference in our anxiety level? We will look at the critical role of developing a healthy attachment to God and deal with some of the obstacles people find along the way. We will also examine contemplative forms of prayer and the differences between Christian and Eastern approaches to meditative prayer.

The names as well as the stories of clients in this book have all been modified so as to preserve their privacy. Each has given permission for their stories to be used as such.

PART I

HOW TO PRAY THROUGH ANXIOUS FEELINGS

Chapter 1

Hope for Relief from Excessive Anxiety

IF YOU WERE TO COME TO ME because you thought you might need the help of a therapist to deal with anxiety, at some point in our sessions I would probably describe to you one or more of the treatments available that we could work on together. We would discuss the pros and cons of each, not to offer you a smorgasbord of options, but to give you hope that there *are* insights and practices that can truly alleviate anxiety while we explore what might be most helpful for you.

However, since we're not talking face to face, I want to share with you some common approaches so you can be more comfortable in seeking the help God has for you. This is not a comprehensive list of therapies but some of the more commonly used.

There are five broad categories. The first is exposure therapies, the second looks at treatments for trauma, the third is about changing the thoughts that lead to anxiety, the fourth is mindfulness, and the fifth is medication. I'll describe them below and address them from a spiritual perspective. We will also do a very quick review of the parts of the brain that are impacted by anxiety so we can refer back to them in later chapters as we see how prayer impacts some of those same areas.

Exposure Therapies

The first and possibly most heavily studied treatment falls under the broad category of exposure. Exposure therapies are all about getting clients to face their anxieties in a controlled way. They aim to keep the client from the two poisons of anxiety: avoidance and reassurance seeking. In order to help the anxious client do this, the therapist first teaches them relaxation exercises to help them get through it. The treatments fall into three groups.

The first is *Systematic Desensitization*, and it involves the client and therapist working together on a plan to increase the exposure slowly over time at a rate that the client is comfortable with. For example, if a client is terrified of riding in an elevator, they would first learn some relaxation techniques. Then they would come up with a multi-step plan. A first step might be imagining being in an elevator. A second step would be standing next to an elevator for two minutes. A third could be pushing the elevator button. A fourth would go as far as waiting for the doors to open, then stepping in and back out. Eventually, they would have a friend go up with them one floor, then two . . . you get the idea. For each of the steps, they need to stay with the anxiety until it dissipates, practicing the relaxation techniques to help them get through it. Allowing the anxiety to increase before it subsides is what makes this technique challenging.

The second and more extreme version of exposure therapy is called *Flooding*. If a client is terrified of driving in parking lots, they might actually have someone drive with them into a parking lot. The driver would then get out of the car and walk away. This would leave the client no choice but to deal with the car in the middle of the lot, so they have to drive their way out of it to get home. Their anxiety would increase a good deal at first, but then it would break.

The third is called *Exposure and Response Prevention*. It is most commonly used with OCD (obsessive compulsive disorder). When a person with OCD locks the door of their house, they may fear that they did not turn the key all the way, or that maybe they forgot, so they seek reassurance by checking it multiple times. Checking may provide short-term relief, but in the long run it does not help anxiety. In fact, it may make it worse. In this example, the exposure part of the treatment is to actually lock the door (and not have their spouse do it, for example, as a way to avoid it); that's the *exposure* part. Then the need to check will be strong, and they will need to resist the urge. That's the *response prevention* part. The anxiety will increase for a short time, but then it will decrease significantly.

Sometimes the very thought of something that causes anxiety, like boarding a plane for someone with a fear of flying, brings about an anxiety response. In that case, we can begin the exposure with the thoughts themselves. We can set a timer and stay with the thought of being on a plane until it is no longer anxiety provoking. This is called *in vitro* desensitization (outside the actual situation), as compared to *in vivo* desensitization (in the situation), which would be actually getting on the plane. That part would then come next.

Exposure therapies need to be maintained in order to keep anxieties from returning. A person with a phobia of airplanes who successfully completes exposure therapy and is able to make several trips, but then begins to avoid flying again, will likely experience relapse. Very often exposure therapy is needed as a first step, however, to bring enough calm to the anxious person that they can deal with underlying root causes—the trauma that may have caused the anxiety in the first place. How God uses exposure therapies and how we respond in prayer, using a Scriptural model, will be the topic of the next chapter.

Therapy for Trauma

Anxiety that results from trauma is generally treated by having the client retell their trauma experience in the caring and supporting presence of a therapist. Working through memories in this way provides empathy that is experienced by the client as a healing agent. Therapists use various techniques to accomplish this. The treatment of choice for many therapists is Eye Movement Desensitization and Reprocessing (EMDR), but not all therapists are trained in it and many employ other techniques. There are ways to pray that can support this process as we work through those memories, and we will cover this in Chapter 6.

Cognitive Restructuring

In many instances, there are thinking patterns that contribute to the anxiety. It is not always an outside stimulus that creates the anxiety. Sometimes it comes from ruminations and thought patterns that make us vulnerable to anxiety. This type of therapy seeks to address that issue through techniques that focus on changing how we think. This is where Scripture can be very helpful, and we will cover this in Chapter 11.

Mindfulness Therapies

Popular and effective treatments for anxiety in recent years include a series of mindfulness-based therapies. Jon Kabat-Zinn, a molecular biologist who studied Zen Buddhism, took Buddhist meditation techniques and used secular language to describe them. He then studied the benefits of these practices and promoted them in the medical community. His work has been well received and proved very effective to many individuals. Forty-one percent of 2,000 mental health professionals surveyed use it as part of their practice.[3]

Kabat-Zinn defines mindfulness as "paying attention in a particular way: on purpose, in the moment, and non-judgmentally. This kind of attention nurtures greater awareness, clarity, and acceptance of present-moment reality."[4] In the realm of mental health, instead of trying to replace negative or distressing thoughts with positive ones, we approach them with curiosity and compassion.[5] This allows us to accept them instead of resisting them. Exercises that promote this goal are many and varied, but the ones of interest to our discussion will focus on breathing, meditation, contemplation, acceptance, and detachment.

There is overlap between some of these practices and prayer practices in some Christian traditions, at least in their potential impact on the brain. There are also differences. These will be explored in Chapters 11 and 12.

Medication

Christians often have some objections to the use of medication for the brain. One of the most common objections is that they fear becoming addicted. This is valid for some medications that are addictive but not for others. Regardless, for this very good reason, it is important to be under the care of a competent and trustworthy medical professional who is licensed to dispense medications appropriately.

The second concern is that somehow we will not be ourselves, that the medication will turn us into someone who is not what God intended us to be. Once again, there is some truth here, but not always. Yes, there are medications that affect our personality. But again, under the proper care, the medication should help us to become more of the people God made us to be, not less of who he made us to be. Interestingly, we rarely hear this concern for people struggling with more severe forms of mental health, like schizophrenia. In those cases, if a medication helps someone who is not in touch with reality to be coherent and recognize clearly what is real and what is not, it is abundantly clear that the person is being more of who God created them to be, not less. It is as if it's acceptable to use chemotherapy to treat cancer but not acceptable to take antibiotics for an infection.

Finally, it is important to recognize that the brain is an organ in the body, and it can have issues like other organs do. And just like other organs are helped by medication, so is the brain. The brain as an organ is something we will now discuss in a bit more detail.

Is It All in Your Head?

Well, the short answer is, no and yes! It's *no* if you imagine anxiety can be cured with the likes of Bobby McFerrin's song from 1988: "Don't Worry, Be Happy." That hit song may have brought a moment of amusement to thousands, but you can't quell real anxiety by telling yourself—or someone else—not to worry. While controlling anxiety can come through realizing there's no reason to worry, that seldom happens instantaneously. And that's because the brain physically changes according to our experiences. And so, in that sense, anxiety *is* in your head.

Neuroscientists formerly thought of the brain as a highly static organ that rarely changed apart from disease. Now they've concluded that the brain is constantly changing and modifying. The brain, it turns out, is not static at all. It can be shaped by negative experiences that are not processed well, like trauma. It can also be shaped by consistent positive activities, just like a bodybuilder can shape and hone muscles to look and perform a certain way. Scientists have not only been able to map out some of the changes anxiety brings, but they've also been able to see some of the positive changes that prayer brings. This can deepen our understanding of how God wants to bless us in our prayer journey, not only to deepen our relationship with him, but also to bring healing in the long run to our anxious minds.

We will look at some of these changes more closely in the discussion in Chapter 11, but for now, let's describe it as simply as this: there is an alarm system in our brain that activates anxiety when it senses danger, and there is also a thinking part that recognizes when the danger is not real and calms down the alarm center. Anxiety can become problematic if the alarm center is overly sensitive, or if the thinking brain is not able to calm it down.

Chapter 2

When God Uses Exposure Therapy

My WIFE AND I MARRIED IN OUR TWENTIES, and over time we had the great blessing and joy of having children. That was a time when the door to anxiety opened more widely in my life. I was so worried about anything happening to my kids. If they coughed once, I feared they were getting bronchitis. A fever with the cough triggered alarms of pneumonia. If it weren't for my wife, I would have been a frequent flyer to the emergency room.

It was completely unhelpful to hear I needed to stop worrying. It was even less helpful for people to tell me I needed to trust God. I had no idea what they meant at the time and found it irritating. It seemed they were speaking a foreign language.

My first attempts at praying through anxiety were mostly prayers for God to keep a laundry list of bad illnesses away from my children and my wife. This basically did not work. I tried to use prayer to get reassurance that bad things would not happen. What I realized eventually was that seeking reassurance beyond a reasonable limit actually increases anxiety. Not only does it not work,[6] but reassurance seeking also reinforces the belief the brain has that there really is something to be concerned about. Praying for health for my kids was reasonable, and I encourage everyone to pray for the health of their loved ones. However, going into excessive detail and lengthy prayers was for me an attempt to control my situation and get additional reassurance beyond what was reasonable.

I got to the point that I no longer told God how I felt or took time to listen to him in my prayer time as I used to do before we had children. My intimacy with God was being hurt. I no longer felt close to him, and the sweetness of my prayer times was drying up. I remember even having a dream during this period where I was trying to eat a meal, but there were so many flies to swat away, I couldn't get the food to my mouth. I believe God was trying to get my attention with that dream, to show me that my preoccupation with praying for each aspect of my anxieties was like swatting at so many flies that it kept me from eating spiritual food.

What I believe was happening in my prayer life was exactly the opposite of systematic desensitization. I was working so hard to get reassurance for my anxiety that it had the effect of increasing the anxiety. Earlier we discussed the effect of seeking reassurance in the example of the person who keeps checking the lock on their door: the anxiety doesn't get better. In fact, it can get worse. If this is an ineffective way to pray, then what is the better way to pray in the face of anxiety?

We know from Scripture that God uses all things for our good. It is safe to say then that the anxiety we are experiencing is going to be used by God for those who love him (Romans 8:28). Knowing that, let's look at how we can pray in ways that are more supportive of what God is doing.

Let's take, for example, a follower of Christ who has a phobia of public speaking and is asked by their boss to make a presentation to a large audience. Whether God—for his own reasons—is bringing this about or not, I believe God can use that opportunity to bring healing, to deepen the person's relationship with him, and to grow their faith. The question then becomes, how would God have them pray about it?

Paul and Jesus

I believe the answer lies in two examples, one from the life of Paul (2 Cor. 12:7-10), and the other from the life of Jesus himself (Mark 14:32-41). Paul complained to God about a thorn in his flesh. He wanted it removed. In the second example, Jesus was facing his coming arrest, torture, and death in Gethsemane. He also asked God to provide another way if possible. The responses from both Paul and Jesus are especially instructive for us. They both discerned that the answer was no. Then they embraced what was to come with hope in how God would redeem it. In Paul's case, he said, "Therefore I will boast all the more gladly about my weaknesses, so that Christ's power may rest on me" (2 Cor. 12:9). For Jesus, we know from Hebrews 12:2 that "for the joy set before him he endured the cross." In the two situations we see an obedience to God that does not involve denial but embraces the suffering and also looks forward with hope to God's redemption.

It is on these responses that we can build a model for prayer in times of anxiety. This model, the *Anxiety Redemption Prayer*, is predicated on a clear understanding of three theological truths that we will explore for the rest of this chapter. The first is an understanding of acceptance of the cross. The second is a deeper embrace of how God is at work to redeem our suffering. The third is a grasp of gratitude in the midst of difficulty.

Acceptance

There is a passage in the Gospel of Luke where Jesus encourages his would-be followers to count the cost of following him. In Luke 14:28-33 he says:

> "Suppose one of you wants to build a tower. Won't you first sit down and estimate the cost to see if you have enough money to complete it? For if you lay the foundation and are not able to finish it, everyone who sees it will ridicule you, saying, 'This person began to build and wasn't able to finish.'
>
> "Or suppose a king is about to go to war against another king. Won't he first sit down and consider whether he is able with ten thousand men to oppose the one coming against him with twenty thousand? If he is not able, he will send a delegation while the other is still a long way off and will ask for terms of peace. In the same way, those of you who do not give up everything you have cannot be my disciples."

In this passage Jesus is clear that we need to be aware that following him has a cost, and it is not small. Jesus' call is one of complete commitment, not a half-hearted one. What is not being addressed in this passage is the cost of *not* following Jesus. Jesus speaks to this elsewhere, giving a very graphic illustration in Matthew 7:24-27:

> "Therefore everyone who hears these words of mine and puts them into practice is like a wise man who built

his house on the rock. The rain came down, the streams rose, and the winds blew and beat against that house; yet it did not fall, because it had its foundation on the rock. But everyone who hears these words of mine and does not put them into practice is like a foolish man who built his house on sand. The rain came down, the streams rose, and the winds blew and beat against that house, and it fell with a great crash."

In my younger Sunday-school-age memories of this parable, I pictured someone building a house on a sandy beach, and someone else building his house up on a cliff where it was rocky ground. In his book *Jesus Through Middle Eastern Eyes*, Dr. Kenneth Bailey explains that Jesus' hearers understood this parable a little differently than I originally had. Jesus' audience knew that in that geographical location, there is a layer of dirt that can be built on, but it is solid only in the summer months when there is no rain in the area. However, when the rainy season comes, the soft soil turns to mud and the house is vulnerable. The prevailing wisdom there is to dig deep enough to get to the rock; in some places a lot of digging is needed and in others the rock is closer to the surface. Regardless of the depth the builder needs to dig to, it will be safe only when he removes all that is in the way of the rock; only then will the foundation for the house be safe in all seasons.[7] Building on sand may seem easy in comparison to digging down to bedrock, but the result is a weak foundation.

If we want a house that can resist wind and rain, we need to dig through our "dirt" until we get to the rock we can build on. If we do what Jesus says, accepting his call to follow him will be costly—it will require digging deeper into our lives. For some of us there will be more sand to dig through than for others, but in the end, the spiritual foundation will be strong enough to withstand the storms of life. Not accepting the cost of discipleship, on the other hand, will weaken our spiritual life and be more costly in the long run.

The value of acceptance when dealing various mental health issues has been demonstrated with the development of a type of therapy called Acceptance and Commitment Therapy. As the title implies, acceptance is an important aspect of that counseling framework. The emphasis is to acknowledge the power of the serenity prayer:[8]

> God grant me the serenity to accept the things I cannot change, the courage to change the things I can, and the wisdom to know the difference.

There is a recognition in this prayer that it takes wisdom to differentiate between the two situations. Acceptance is not about passivity, it is not about giving up or giving in, and it is not a failure. Rather it is an intentional choice to face what is difficult and cannot be changed, with the understanding that there is a benefit in not avoiding it.[9] A review of studies related to the effectiveness of Acceptance and Commitment Therapy was conducted by Steven Hayes (et al.) in 2005. He identified several studies that looked specifically at the effectiveness of acceptance in reducing the distress of anxiety. Not only was there an impact, but it was also noted to be unusually large for the behavioral sciences.[10]

One somewhat tricky aspect of acceptance in the face of anxiety is the distinction between (1) acceptance of the feared event, (2) acceptance of its remote possibility, and

(3) acceptance of the anxiety itself. If the fear is so great, but the possibility of the event is remote, the acceptance of the event itself may be so difficult that it is worth taking a step back and working instead on accepting the remote possibility of the event. A step further back would be to accept the anxiety itself. This alone is often very helpful both spiritually and psychologically. Spiritually, we are saying what Paul said—that we embrace our weakness looking forward to God's power in transforming it. Psychologically we are reaping the benefit described by Steven Hayes and his team.

In addition to the Serenity Prayer described above, there is another spiritual practice that is mainly focused on acceptance once we have discerned what is God's call. It's called the Prayer of Welcome. This prayer goes to the root of our basic needs for love, security, and a sense of agency or control. It is done in four movements:

1. Jesus, I let go of my need to be safe and secure. Welcome.
2. Jesus, I let go of my need to be accepted and approved of. Welcome.
3. Jesus, I let go of my need to control this person or event. Welcome.
4. Jesus, I let go of my need to change reality and receive it as it is. Welcome.[11]

Redemption

After my wife and I were married in 1988, we lived in the Chicago area. We knew we wanted to have a lot of kids, so we got started right away. We had three boys, and then we became pregnant with our first daughter. My job at the time required a lot of travel to Dallas, where the company had a facility I usually worked in. If my wife needed me, she had a number where I could be reached. But on one occasion, the meeting involved many people, and the facility did not have a conference room large enough, so we rented a large room at a different location.

I was checking my voicemails during the breaks from a payphone (yes, this was before cellphones; we used to call and retrieve the voicemails people had left us) and found a message from my wife. She had had a routine doctor's appointment for a pregnancy checkup that day and had been trying to reach me because she had some bad news. But because the company meeting was off site, she couldn't reach anyone at my work, and she had no way to contact me.

My beloved wife was sitting alone with scary news, trying to get hold of me. While on the phone listening to her panicked voicemail, I overheard some people getting a cab to the airport to catch an early flight home before the meeting was over. I immediately caught a ride with them and got home on the earliest standby flight available. The doctor had said something was wrong, and we needed to get a second-level ultrasound to find out more detail. That second ultrasound revealed devastating news. So many things were wrong with the baby that there was only a 50 percent chance she would be born alive. Even if she was born alive, the chances of her surviving the first year of life were around 10 percent!

My wife carried our baby Grace until the eighth month of pregnancy, when Grace died in utero and was stillborn. As you can imagine, this was a time of deep grief for us. I was already dealing with anxiety, so it was hard for me, but losing the baby was especially difficult for my wife.

I was struggling with how to trust God in the middle of my anxieties, and my wife had been a role model for me of someone who trusted God much better than I did. But in this circumstance, her trust in God was also shaken. So we made a lovely pair as we struggled to learn what it was like to trust God.

One day during this period, we were driving south on I-294 and needed to pass through a toll booth by O'Hare Airport. This was before the days of automatic transponders, and I didn't have change to throw in the manual lane basket. As we pulled up to the booth with an attendant, my wife and I were in the middle of a passionate theological and highly personal discussion about what it really meant for us to trust God and, frankly, whether we could.

As we reached the booth, I handed the attendant a dollar bill with my left hand, my face still turned toward my wife as we continued our discussion. But the attendant wouldn't take my money. I looked back at her a bit irritated. She pointed to the car ahead of us and said, "She paid for you!" The generous driver ahead of us had paid our toll, but the words "paid for you" hung in the air as if they'd been shouted from a megaphone. It was a small gift, but I was stunned. It was clear to me God was reminding us that the reason we can trust him is that Jesus "paid for us" when he died for our sins.

I share this story because I think the Cross is at the center of what we need to talk about next. Jesus calls us to accept the cross he gives us; there is no doubt about that. But there is more to the Cross than suffering. The Cross leads to resurrection. The Resurrection is the ultimate redemption. In the simplest terms, it is the power to turn something awful into something very good. What I've found over the years is that we had a very anemic view of redemption, partly due to immaturity in our faith journeys. It was also due to an incomplete understanding of what God is saying to us and modeling for us in the Scriptures.

My first exposure to the idea of God's redemption was in college. A classmate told me how her breakup experience helped her relate to another friend going through her own breakup. This was an example of a common perspective among modern Christians, that somehow God can bring something good out of a difficult situation, but it is limited to that particular genre of difficulty. If a young adult loses a parent, they are better equipped to comfort another young adult going through a similar grief. Scripture also tells us that God uses suffering to strengthen our character, to purify us, and to make us kinder and more loving people. Yet another view of redemption tends to come from a secular direction. It is well encapsulated in the sayings "look for the silver lining" or "look for the positive" in suffering. All the above are true, but they are incomplete.

When Jesus went to the Cross, God did not say, "Okay, Son, the good thing is now that you know what it feels like to be crucified, you can really help others who are being crucified." To some extent this is indeed true—God has entered our suffering and shares in it. This is a powerful theological truth. It is a comfort in our own suffering to know that Jesus also suffered. However, there was a much greater benefit to the Cross, and that was the supernatural power of the Resurrection. Jesus' death and resurrection made possible the release of the Holy Spirit (John 16:7). And it is the Holy Spirit who gives all Christians the spiritual power to be in relationship with God.

In a smaller way, as each of us suffers for the sake of God's calling on our lives, as Jesus did for his, we experience the same spiritual phenomenon Paul describes as sharing in the suffering of Christ (Rom. 8:17; 2 Cor. 1:5; 4:7-18; Gal. 6:17; Phil. 1:29; 3:8-10; Col. 1:24;1 Thess. 1:6; 3:2-3). When we do so, we are given some measure of resurrection. There may be no discernable feelings associated with this spiritual phenomenon, but its reality is evident in the new life that we experience at a later date. It is also manifested in our ability to be of benefit to others. We are given more spiritual power to help others in our ministries as a result of sharing in the suffering of Christ. (Suffering that seems unrelated to our calling will be addressed later in this chapter.)

I believe it is for that reason that we learn more from teachers who have suffered than those who have not. We don't know exactly how that works, but I know my life has been more impacted and changed by mentors and teachers who have experienced suffering than those who have not.

Elizabeth and Jim Elliott went to be missionaries to the unreached Wuaorani indigenous people group in Ecuador in the 1950s. Jim Elliott, along with four other missionaries, was killed by the Wuaorani as they first encountered each other. Elizabeth Elliott's grief and suffering had a powerful impact on her later years of ministry. She went back to the tribe that had killed her husband, and many of them subsequently became followers of Christ. Even after she came back to the United States, her ministry continued to be highly influential. I remember learning from her how God uses suffering in our lives even when I was not really in agreement or attracted to some of her views on other theological issues.

I'm sure you're not surprised that there is much more in the New Testament about suffering. Paul, especially, seems to indicate that as we share in the suffering of

Christ, we are given additional power in our ministry. We not only become more like Christ because we suffer like him and learn humility and obedience to God, but we also become like Jesus in his power to bless others.

Let's look at 2 Corinthians, where Paul makes this explicit in two passages. First, in 2 Corinthians 1:3-7 we read:

> Praise be to the God and Father of our Lord Jesus Christ, the Father of compassion and the God of all comfort, who comforts us in all our troubles, so that we can comfort those in any trouble with the comfort we ourselves receive from God. For just as we share abundantly in the sufferings of Christ, so also our comfort abounds through Christ. If we are distressed, it is for your comfort and salvation; if we are comforted, it is for your comfort, which produces in you patient endurance of the same sufferings we suffer. And our hope for you is firm, because we know that just as you share in our sufferings, so also you share in our comfort.

And a bit later in 2 Corinthians 4:10-12 Paul writes:

> We always carry around in our body the death of Jesus, so that the life of Jesus may also be revealed in our body. For we who are alive are always being given over to death for Jesus' sake, so that his life may also be revealed in our mortal body. So then, death is at work in us, but life is at work in you.

In a more general sense, as we embrace other suffering that God allows in our lives, whether related to our living out the Gospel or not, we are also sharing in the sufferings of Christ. We tend to think of Jesus' suffering as the crucifixion and Paul's suffering as the persecution he endured.

However, Romans 8:28-29 tells us that the scope of God's redemption is much wider:

> And we know that in all things God works for the good of those who love him, who have been called according to his purpose. For those God foreknew he also predestined to be conformed to the image of his Son, that he might be the firstborn among many brothers and sisters.

Notice that in this famous passage Paul says God uses *all things* and that *all things* are used to make us more like Jesus—and being like Jesus means what? It means our suffering creates benefit for others. It's the kind of theology that enables us to see why Paul can be thankful for suffering. It's not because he likes suffering, but because he experiences a greater power of God for himself and for others as God redeems the suffering.

In summary then, my suffering not only teaches me to become more kind, patient, and loving like Christ, it also gives me more of Christ's power to bless others through my ministry. Knowing that God is redeeming things is critical to how we view suffering. And changing how we view suffering is critical to handling anxiety differently. This may feel like small comfort to someone who is in the middle of tremendous pain and anxiety. I have been there. At times I have told God I didn't care how Christlike he was making me. I didn't care how much effectiveness and power he was going to later give me to bless others as a result, I just wanted the suffering to end. If that's how you feel, I don't think God wants you to beat yourself up. Rather, continue to press into him by telling him how you feel, and work through the sections of this book on trauma.

The Power of Gratitude

Regardless of how bad the situation is, we know from the above discussion that God is working to redeem it. How God plans to redeem the situation is rarely clear in the moment. However, since we know God redeems our life and life experiences, we can have faith that this redemption will be good. We therefore have that redemption to look forward to. This redemption is something we can be grateful for even before we can envision how it will work out.

I have known some individuals and some Christian traditions that have such a strong conviction of the coming redemption of any difficulty, including anxiety, that they are even grateful *for* the difficulty itself. While I understand the motivation to be grateful for it because of the coming redemption, I find it often takes an additional level of faith I don't have. Moreover, being told to be grateful for the difficulty *itself* seems to invalidate the pain we are experiencing. To illustrate how this feels, imagine a well-meaning Christian telling their suffering friend: "It must be God's will that this terrible thing has happened. Thank him for it." For me, the distinction between being grateful for the redemption and not the difficulty is helpful. In some ways it feels to me that when something bad happens and out of faith we rename it as good, we are not being authentic. I find a resistance in me to proclaiming something *bad* to be *good*.

The value of gratitude in mental health has been documented in numerous studies and included as an area of study in positive psychology, a branch that focuses on what makes life good and healthy rather than on mental illness.[12] Studies that focused on gratitude journals showed that they prompted improvements in well-being,[13] leading to the use of such journals by mental health professionals.

In one study of 83 Chinese adults in Hong Kong over sixty years old, the fear and anxiety over death was studied. One group was given a gratitude task, another a task focusing on their hassles, and a third a neutral task. The group with the gratitude task showed the least anxiety. In the background section of that research paper, they noted an inverse link between fear of death and acceptance of it.[14] That link between gratitude and acceptance was not studied in that research, but it is an important one, and will be part ofthe Anxiety Redemption Prayer described in the next chapter.

On a physiological level, a brain imaging study that looked at brains experiencing gratitude showed that there was increased brain activity in the *anterior cingulate cortex*,[15] the part of the brain that is also involved in regulating emotions. Dr. Karl Lehman, in his book *Outsmarting Yourself*, describes a sequence of events that begins with being appreciative, which then releases the hormone oxytocin. This hormone predisposes us for healthy attachment and emotional bonding and positive relational connection.[16] When we apply that same sequence to prayer, we can see that the exercise of gratitude creates fertile ground for a solid personal connection with God in the midst of anxiety.

Chapter 3

Anxiety Redemption Prayer

EARLIER THIS YEAR I HAD A PHYSICAL, and I received results from my doctor that my PSA levels had risen too fast since the last test, and he wanted to refer me to a urologist. I got the referral but had to wait a few months for the next available appointment. In the meantime, I did some initial research and was reassured to find that in most cases, the PSA level I had was not all that worrisome. I wish I had not looked any further. Because as I looked for more reassurance, I started to find scarier and scarier things about painful biopsies, side effects of surgeries, and so on. Needless to say, that increased my anxiety. I came to God with my anxiety.

In this chapter, I want to explore what that looks like— to bring our anxieties to God in the time of our distress. So, here is a model for praying through anxiety that includes four basic steps:

1. Pray for God to fix the problem.
2. If it seems he is not fixing it, express gratitude for how he is redeeming it.
3. Pray for how he is redeeming it.

4. Accept the situation. If that is still difficult, pray for strength and courage to endure and to accept it.

Step 1: Pray for God to fix the problem

One pattern we see in the Gospels is that when Jesus was presented with suffering, his most consistent response was to heal. The Christian response to suffering throughout the centuries always begins with working to alleviate the suffering. That is our first step. If someone is sick, the first things we do are take them to a doctor and pray for healing. We shouldn't say, "Press into Jesus in your suffering and take courage because God is redeeming it," until after we have done everything *we* can do to relieve the suffering.

Step 2: Gratitude for redemption instead

The Bible is clear that God does not always take away suffering. When he does not take it away, we don't need to presume that God doesn't love us or that we have somehow failed. Instead, we can shift our attention by faith to God's redemption of the negative circumstance. However, the truth is that in the middle of difficulty, I don't always find that I'm able to thank God for my circumstances. I only find it doable within the level of faith I've been given to believe God is working to redeem the situation. This is especially true since I've come to the conclusions described in the previous chapter regarding how redemption works. Knowing that he is at work to redeem a bad situation, I can begin to thank God for that redemption. That helps me to remember God's sovereignty, that he is still in charge, and it begins to reduce the anxiety.

This step has two benefits, one psychological and the other spiritual. The psychological benefit is that gratitude will bring about some calm. The spiritual benefit is that it will engender faith that God is at work and not absent from the situation. As we saw earlier about how the brain functions, gratitude engages the cingulate cortex, which is involved in calming the amygdala. It also releases oxytocin, which predisposes us for positive relational connection. This is especially needed since the natural tendency for many of us in that moment is to feel a negative relational connection toward God. This application of gratitude to calm anxiety is also seen in Philippians 4:6-7: "Do not be anxious about anything, but in every situation, by prayer and petition, with thanksgiving, present your requests to God. And the peace of God, which transcends all understanding, will guard your hearts and your minds in Christ Jesus." I wonder if Paul knew about the cingulate cortex.

Step 3: Pray for how God is redeeming it

The next step in the model reinforces the sense of faith that is beginning to develop. It elevates the anticipation of redemption even more. We generally do not know how God will redeem suffering when we are in the midst of it. Sometimes our friends and those near us can see how the redemption may come, but most of the time we can't see it, and no one really knows God's plans for redemption before he brings it about. This is challenging because it is so unclear in the present, and we are usually in too much pain to keep our eyes on the future. One thing I have found helpful in this is to pray for how God is redeeming the situation. Since we know he is using it for good, we can pray for that good. We can pray for all that he is doing even though we do not know what that is. This helps to reinforce yet again that God is not absent and that he is working in the midst of our pain and anxiety.

What's even more helpful is to remember that the suffering is not wasted and that our suffering has benefit. People can endure suffering much more easily when they sense there is a purpose to it. This is the essence of the psychiatrist Dr. Viktor Frankl's observations in his book *Man's Search for Meaning*. A survivor of Auschwitz, he noted that those who had a purpose, a task waiting for them, were more likely to survive the camps, and that this observation was replicated in Japanese, North Korean, and North Vietnamese prisoner of war camps.[17] Praying in this way helps us to hang on to God's purpose for our lives, to make us more like Jesus.

Step 4: Embrace acceptance and pray for strength and courage

The last step of this prayer is to embrace acceptance. If that is still difficult, we can pray for the strength and courage to endure and to accept the suffering. The cross is part of the journey, and it is important to embrace that truth. When I first began following Christ seriously as an adult, I did not understand this. I thought that if I did all the right things, God would help me out and get my life on track. God did indeed help me out, and he did put my life back on track, but it was his track, not the track I had in mind.

Part of that process was understanding that suffering was part of the journey and that there was no way to avoid it. When I accepted this, it was a step toward freedom from anxiety. I remember wrestling with anxious thoughts and wondering, if the worst-case scenario was what God wanted, could I accept it? Well, I thought, Jesus is the one I follow. I've decided this a long time ago. Nothing has changed; I still want to follow him. If following him means I will not have the life I wanted, then that's that; nothing has really changed. This is also true when the thing I'm having trouble accepting is the anxiety itself. I have found it helpful to recognize that God is redeeming that suffering, and I can be thankful for that redemption.

One episode of anxiety I experienced in my career was during a period of layoffs. I knew that if I was laid off, it would interfere with and significantly delay my plans to move toward a second career. I felt I was called to a life revolving around care for people emotionally and spiritually in various ways, like counseling, spiritual direction, mentoring, teaching, and writing. I had gone to school for more than a decade part-time to achieve that goal. The worst-case scenario in that case would have been a multi-year delay in making the career moves I had planned and looked forward to for such a long time. As I wrestled with that anxiety, I was greatly helped to accept that if God wanted to delay my plans, then ultimately, I wanted what he wanted. It's what I had signed up for by following him.

I'm not saying that coming to acceptance of suffering is easy, not by a long shot; it's probably the hardest thing to do. But when we are having difficulty accepting these worst-case possibilities, or the anxieties themselves, that is where the hope for redemption comes in. We can trust that God is doing something bigger and better through our suffering. Now that requires faith, and if we don't have enough faith, we can ask for the faith we need to accept what is ahead.

An Example of How to Use the Prayer

Going back to my experience with the elevated PSA levels, here's an example of how I used this prayer model:

1. *Jesus, I am not worried about dying, I am most anxious about the biopsies; I hear they're painful. I'm anxious about the treatments too, and some of the awful side effects.* Then I prayed for God to take it away completely: *I pray, Lord, that the next time they check my PSA levels, they will be back to normal.*

The next step is the one where I had to accept in faith that God was using this for good and thank him for it. As described earlier, I know a lot of people thank God for the suffering itself. I don't have that kind of faith; maybe you do. But it's hard enough for me to thank God for the redemption, so this is what I prayed:

2. *Thank you, Lord, for how you are redeeming this. I know you are using it for good somehow, and I thank you for that ahead of time.*

The next step was to pray for what God is doing:

3. *Lord, I want to pray for redemption. I want to pray and ask for the fullness of the good you are bringing out of this.*

Finally, the last step was to be able to accept the suffering, whatever it might be.

4. *Lord, I don't know yet what is going on, but I accept the suffering of not knowing at this point. Give me the grace to be calm and strength to endure.*

The next time they did the PSA test, it was back to normal levels. So, of course, I thanked God that in this case he chose to take it away.

A Sample Prayer for You to Try

1. Identify as clearly as you can what you are anxious about, and write it down in detail. Spend some time praying that God would take away what is anxiety provoking.

Lord, I'm very afraid that _____. I pray that as much anxiety (or cause of anxiety) as can be taken from me within your will, you would take it from me.

2. If God is not taking it away, thank him ahead of time for how he intends to redeem it.
   a. Remember, we said that no matter what is going on, we know that God is redeeming it; he is somehow using it to make us more like Jesus.
   b. Expressing gratitude helps to calm us down and builds our faith that God is active and the world is not out of control.

Lord, I acknowledge that you are at work to redeem this somehow. Even though I don't know how, I have faith that you are redeeming it, and I thank you.

3. Pray for that redemption, even though you don't know how that will happen. This reinforces our faith that God is at work.

Lord, it is hard to know how you are redeeming this or using it for good for me and for others. But I know that you are doing that, so I pray for whatever it is that you are doing, that you would bring about the fullness of your will in and through this situation.

4. Pray for the faith to accept the particular suffering and to accept that God is bringing good out of it.

Lord, I accept the suffering you have not taken away, and I accept the suffering of not knowing at this point what you will or will not take away or how you are using it all for good. I pray that you will help me to be calm in the midst of this storm, and that you give me the strength to endure.

Chapter 4

Counting the Cost of Avoiding the Cross

REBECCA WAS A CLIENT WHO CAME TO ME SUFFERING from anxiety. She had taken a less prestigious job because her previous job had triggered her anxieties too much. But her new job forced her to travel, and she also had phobias associated with travel. However, the more she avoided travel, the worse it got.

As I worked with her, she acknowledged she wanted a better job, and once she saw how her avoidance was causing greater misery, she determined to face it. As she began to take small steps to face her anxiety and began the process of traveling for the interviews, she was eventually offered the better job. Of course, the new job also required travel, which she began to have victory after victory in facing, one small step at a time. I had explained to her that the anxiety would increase at first, but if she stayed with it, it would decrease and go away. To her great credit, she accepted the initial pain of the increased anxiety and began to reap the rewards. She began to see a pattern of success that motivated her to keep going. If she had continued her pattern of avoidance, it may have seemed easier initially, but her anxiety and depression would likely have only worsened.

The Cross and Exposure Therapy

As we discussed earlier, acceptance of the cross—that is, acceptance of suffering—is part of following Jesus. It should not be surprising that doing the opposite—resisting the cross—creates problems both spiritually and psychologically. Spiritually, whenever we resist God's desire for us, it creates tension in our relationship with him. This tension is not because God is withdrawing love from us, but rather due to our turning away from his love.

Psychologically, resisting suffering can be an example of avoidance. In Chapter 1, we talked about how avoidance creates more anxiety. Though temporary relief may tempt us, the cost of avoidance becomes higher than embracing the cross. Jesus said as much: if we try to hang on to our lives, we will lose them (Mark 10:39). The depth of that statement by Jesus is hard to fathom at times, but it is a fundamental experiential truth of following him that we will discuss further in Chapter 5.

It is tempting at times to feel that God is being unfair and capricious in making us face anxiety. However, we have already described how exposure therapy is an established method of reducing anxiety. When we take steps to face our anxieties, they diminish. When we avoid them, on the other hand, they tend to get worse. When we pray for God to take away the source of an anxiety and he does not, there is a strong possibility he is bringing about healing by helping us to face it. I can't, of course, get into the mind of God, but I can give you my best guess. It seems to me that much of the time if God does not take away our anxiety, it is because he wants us to grow by facing it. If a therapist can help a client by guiding them through exposure therapies, why wouldn't God, the ultimate therapist, do the same?

In addition to breaking the power of anxiety by facing it, God is helping us grow spiritually. With each instance, if we believe God's invitation is best for us, as we step into it and see positive fruit, our faith increases. One might argue that one's faith is really in the exposure therapy, rather than in God. For many that may indeed be the case. However, when we bring the anxiety-provoking situation to God in prayer and face it *with* him, it nurtures our faith in God as well.

There are times when doing this can be difficult, not because of the anxiety itself, but because the anxiety is so general, we don't know exactly what it is we are anxious about. Then it's hard to pray specifically about it or act on it. In those cases, it's helpful to talk through it with someone, preferably a mental health professional.

Quick-Acting "Medicine"

Generally, the clients I see in counseling who try exposure therapy find rewards and relief faster than they expect. Exposure therapy can be excruciatingly difficult. However, one piece of good news is that it can be surprisingly fast-acting medicine. It's as if there's an underlying anxiety mechanism in the brain whereby beliefs and cognitive reassurances are only valid once we act upon them. When we act upon them, our brain says, "Yes, this is true, no need to be anxious."

I will share one story from my experience that illustrates how fast-acting exposure therapy can be. One time when my boys were young, our church sponsored a back-to-school campout. Wall climbing was just becoming popular, and the campground had erected a forty-foot tower with climbing options all around. The boys were excited about it, of course, but they also knew I did not like heights.

Still, I did not want to set an example of giving in to fear. I decided I was going to face my fear and climb that tower. The guy giving instructions told me that the equipment for rappelling down the tower was strong enough to carry the weight of a small car. So, my brain knew that it was safe, but that didn't change how I *felt*. The brain can know the anxiety is irrational but still be anxious.

Well, I didn't look down. I kept my eyes straight up as I climbed all the way to the top, with anxiety in my gut the whole time.

When I began to rappel down, after one bounce, I realized, "Oooh, this is safe, and it's fun!" and all the anxiety disappeared. My brain believed my action and experience of trusting the equipment far more than any reassurance from the instructor that it was strong enough to hold a car. I went on to climb the rest of the walls up to the level of difficulty my middle-aged muscles could handle.

Pursuing Reassurance

The other thing I noticed about fears related to health is that when I try to get reassurance, there is a point where the anxieties get worse. I mentioned earlier my anxiety around my PSA levels. At the time, I did some initial research and learned some useful things. But I've come to realize there is always a line in these things. If I cross it—if I try to know too much without being a medical doctor—I will feel even more anxious. Sure enough, I was initially reassured. That first assurance, a seeking to understand reality, is good. But as I kept going, as I went past what a non-anxious person would normally do, I found things that made me a lot more anxious. And not being a physician, I couldn't put them in perspective.

Part of what happens is that we train our minds to believe the answer to anxiety is more reassurance, but the problem is that the need for reassurance doesn't lessen, it gets worse. When we resist seeking unnecessary reassurance, we are on the right track. As we resist, the anxiety may get worse at first, but that initial spike in anxiety decreases to the point where it is far better than where we started, and that particular anxiety loses its power.

Sometimes it's not easy to know when it is appropriate to face an anxious situation or if there is wisdom in avoiding it because of actual danger. I have found that the best way to handle that kind of circumstance is to ask someone you trust who does not struggle with anxiety, at least not with anxiety around the same things you do. For instance, a friend of mine and I went out to lunch, and a piece of chicken fell from my plate onto the table. My friend knows about my health anxieties, so I asked him if it was reasonable for me to eat it or not. He thought the table was clean enough, so even though I didn't want to, I stuffed it in my mouth.

A similar situation happened several years ago with my smartphone. I know millennials make fun of my generation because some of us carried our phones on our belts, but it worked, usually. On this occasion, the holster on my belt was a clip on, and the phone slipped off and fell on the floor face down in a public restroom, right next to the urinal.

You can imagine this was not easy for me. I had to figure out just how much rubbing alcohol was okay to clean it with without ruining the device. I once again had to call my friend and say, "Hey, this is how much cleaning I did, is it reasonable for me to stop now?" Then I had to, of course, resist the temptation of more rounds of alcohol wiping and take the necessary next step of putting it to my face. Good news, I survived!

Remote Possibility versus High Probability

There is one additional insight into the nature of anxiety that is worth mentioning at this point. Most of the time when we are dealing with anxiety, the things we are anxious about are remote possibilities. The problem is that our brain treats them as being much more probable.

When my children were young, one of them read a children's book about volcanoes and earthquakes, and it scared him. He asked me if we lived on a fault line. The reality is that we do live on a fault line, but it's a dormant one. I explained that no significant seismic activity had happened for a hundred years or more, but that did nothing to reassure him. He understood cognitively what I was saying, but the emotional part of his brain was still believing that it was a high-probability event rather than a remote one. Once the door of possibility was open to a perceived threat in his mind, his brain was treating it as much more probable than it was.

Many of us do this with anxiety to some degree or another. Sometimes we can tell when it's irrational, other times we cannot. Whether we can tell it's irrational or not does not always make a difference. It is very common for anxiety to persist even when we know cognitively that the probability of danger is extremely remote. When it comes to acceptance in this case, it may be better to shift the focus of acceptance to the anxiety itself, because the level of acceptance of the remote possibility might be out of reach for many, and it is not a realistic threat of any sort anyway.

Prayer Modifiers

When we are not clear on what is making us anxious even after talking with someone about our feelings, we can also ask God for clarity. It is also helpful to ask God for help in putting things in the right perspective. Asking God to help us see how unlikely something is, both cognitively and emotionally, can be helpful. We can pray that our emotional assessment of danger realistically matches the possibility of it coming to pass. Finally, it also makes sense to ask for the strength needed to successfully do the exposure work. One way to modify the Anxiety Redemption Prayer from Chapter 3 is to add requests to cover these themes.

Sample Prayer Modifications

Step 1: In this first step, if you experience difficulty identifying what you are anxious about, ask God to show you more clearly. Then take the time to journal and write down as much as you know about your anxiety. When you have identified the root anxiety or anxieties, you can proceed with step 1 of asking God to take away the cause of your anxiety.

Step 2: In this step, as you express gratitude for God's redemption, if it's not enough to bring calm, begin to pray for truth to replace any lies you may be believing. Since most anxious thoughts result from wrong perceptions, as we described earlier, pray for perspective.

Step 3: This step can proceed with no modification, praying for God's redemption.

Step 4: In the last step, as you express acceptance and pray for calm and strength to endure, remember that you can also pray for grace to accept the anxiety itself. Finally, pray for strength not to give in to any reassurance-seeking behaviors if that's a temptation.

Chapter 5

Social Anxiety, Social Media, and Self-Acceptance

JAMIE CAME TO SEE ME BECAUSE HER PARENTS FELT it was a good idea for her to get some help with her shyness. She had graduated from college, but aside from her job she was very homebound. She avoided social interactions assiduously. But Jamie actually wanted to be with people and was energized by them, so her isolation was especially painful.

Her anxiety had developed in her early teen years when she had experienced some bullying, began to withdraw from others, and stayed close with the friends and family she already knew and trusted. She dreaded graduating high school because of the fear of what going away to college would mean in terms of meeting new people and having to make new friends. Fortunately, college worked out well for her. Her roommate was kind and accepting and helped draw her into a new social circle with whom she became very close. But although she was interested in dating, and one guy in particular was interested in her, she was just too shy to respond. Now that she had graduated, she stayed in contact long distance with her friends, but otherwise stayed at home and continued to avoid all social interactions.

Social anxiety is a fear of social situations and interactions. At its core, it is usually about anticipation of shame.[18] It can involve fear of rejection, fear of embarrassment, and so on. Its impact on the social interactions of the individual is costly because it creates a loss of community as they avoid social interactions more and more. One study has shown that the brain's alarm system, the amygdala, in people who suffer from social anxiety is much more activated when the subjects are shown images of faces with negative expressions. The stronger the anxiety symptoms of the subject, the more the amygdala shows reactivity to the negative expressions.[19] They essentially react to the *possibility* of social threat with heightened alarm.

People with social anxiety have a higher chance of developing other anxiety and mood disorders,[20] so it is important to try to address this issue earlier rather than later. Mindfulness as well as cognitive-based therapies have been shown to be helpful for social anxiety.[21] Mindfulness will be discussed in Chapters 11 and 12. This chapter, however, deals with the cognitive aspects of how our relationship with God can help us reformulate how we feel about various social situations that may have otherwise been anxiety provoking.

The Effects of Social Media

In current sociological trends, levels of social anxiety are often related to use of social media. The relationship between social media and social anxiety is hard to measure, yet a number of studies have shown that there is a relationship. In 2016, a review of twenty studies on the subject showed that only four of them failed to establish a relationship between the two. Some of the clearer findings involve associations between problematic or addictive social media use and social anxiety.[22] Another study found that addictive social media use was associated not only with social anxiety but also with lower happiness levels.[23]

Among young people, social media creates a way of measuring social success with metrics such as the number of online "friends" and positive or negative responses.[24] An increase in social anxiety can develop if they keep checking their postings to see how many "likes" they receive and compare their "scores" with those of their peers. When they do this, they are in effect seeking reassurance for their anxiety over whether or not they are accepted by their peers. This makes sense from the point of view of avoidance and exposure therapy. When they check the number of likes (seeking reassurance), they increase their anxiety levels.

Fortunately, the exposure treatments described in earlier chapters work well for social anxiety, and they work equally well for in-person social situations and online social media interactions. The most straightforward answer to social anxiety is to continually expose oneself to social situations and not avoid them. The more we avoid them, the worse the anxiety is the next time around. The more we confront it, the less anxiety we have the next time. This is not the whole answer, but it is a very significant part of the road to recovery from this socially isolating condition.

Jamie and I began to work on this by reviewing some of her beliefs and planning for systematic desensitization. We planned for small conversations, at first setting small goals that she could achieve. She began by visiting a singles ministry at her church but did not stay long. This was followed by staying through a whole event. Then she moved on to joining a small group. This was a big step and felt like a huge victory because it opened up a chance to do social things with the small group. Jamie is a very likeable person, and soon she was being invited to multiple events. She was at first anxious to attend, but as she did so, she discovered that exposure therapy does work, and that her fears disappeared. In parallel with the exposure therapy, Jamie explored with me the painful feelings of high school and moving to college and found a measure of healing and comfort around those memories. At the same time, she also began to grow deeper in her relationship with God. She drew on her deepening relationship with him and began to ask him for the strength to face her anxieties. This gave her the strength to push herself even more and pursue additional opportunities to face anxiety. She has also recently begun dating someone for the first time in her life.

But Jamie's story does include some setbacks. There were opportunities for facing her anxieties that she chose not to take. However, with God's help, she has done well. Of course, not all who suffer from social anxiety have as straightforward a path as Jamie's. For some there may be core beliefs to tackle, the need to help the person reinterpret social cues, and so on. There are also a few spiritual and psychological subtleties to social anxiety that are worth exploring in this chapter.

Seeking Reassurance on Social Media

Let's say I just posted something on a social media platform, and I feel vulnerable. Actually, that's a real-life example for me. I use an Instagram account to post about some fictional writing I do at myspiritualdirector.com. Every few weeks I post an entry in the form of a letter from a spiritual director to a directee. Naturally, I want to know that the post is doing well and generating many likes. If I check often, the act of checking reinforces in my brain that there is something to be concerned about. The more I check, the higher my anxiety level becomes. The more I don't check, however, the more reassuring it is to my brain that there is nothing to worry about. I can rationalize all I want cognitively that it's okay to check, but my brain will believe my action, and my action of checking says there is indeed something to worry about. The brain will believe that action so much more than cognitive rationalizations.

There is a deeper spiritual dimension to this as well. When I don't check my post, I am exercising faith muscles—not faith that there will be a record number of likes, but faith that God can use my post for even one person who needs it . . . or even for me. This exercise of my faith muscle will help my faith grow. I am teaching myself to believe that God is in charge of the outcome, and it strengthens my faith in his sovereignty. Not only that, but the deeper lesson here is that I am training myself to accept God's will for me even if it is not my own will for myself.

That's a very small example, but the same is true with the PSA test that I shared about earlier. There's a point at which I have taken all necessary precautions, I've made the right appointments, I've done a reasonable amount of research, and I need to let go and leave it in God's hands. When I am able to do that, the anxiety may get worse for a while before it gets better, but praying at that point helps my faith grow as I resist the urge to control more than is possible by seeking more reassurance.

Experiencing Shame as Trauma

One theory as to how social anxiety disorder develops is that for some children with a shy temperament, experiences of shame or embarrassment are amplified. If the experiences are repeated over time, they can be experienced as a series of very small traumas (see a working definition of small traumas in Chapter 6). This in turn creates a heightened sensitivity to any form of perceived social threat.[25] Because the person is hypervigilant and focused on negative social cues, they may miss positive social cues. Therapy needs to focus on helping them to reinterpret social cues more correctly, as well as focus on both exposure therapy and the underlying small traumas. Similarly, in prayer, it would be worth praying for truth in interpreting social cues, exercising the Anxiety Redemption Prayer discussed in the last two chapters, and considering the chapters in this book that address prayer in support of healing work on smaller trauma.

Social Anxiety and Self-Acceptance

Finally, I want to address a type of anxiety related to self-acceptance. One thing I have found difficult at times is to accept that I said something embarrassing. Maybe at a meeting I made a foolish comment, or my suggestion was outright rejected. I would typically do whatever I could to push that thought away. The problem is that the more I try to push the unpleasant thought away, the more it pushes back.

In a psychological sense, that's feeding the anxiety. Mindfulness therapy, which we will discuss in Chapter 11, would say that the best thing is to acknowledge the anxiety, be curious about it, and not fight with it. This is better than trying to tell myself, "Oh, it's not as bad as you think" or "Don't worry, no one will remember it." Those thoughts are equivalent to seeking reassurance. Instead, mindfulness would say we should just accept it but not engage with it, like a cloud in the sky you can't do much about, and let it pass. Not engaging with it is more effective than grappling with it, that's for sure, but in Christ we can go further and get to the root of the problem.

The root of the problem is pride. I want to see myself as being too good to have made such a mistake. That kind of pride makes the thought of that mistake unacceptable to me, so I need to push back on that thought, which of course makes the thought have even more energy. Instead, if I bring that pride to Jesus in repentance, I can find a healing that is guaranteed to remove the sting of the mistake. It's as if the darkness that attaches itself to my pride cannot remain when the full light of the humility of Christ shines there. The way to pray about that is simple, but in case you do not have the words for it, try something like this sample prayer:

> *Lord, I repent of the pride that keeps me from accepting that I could be someone who . . . _____.*
> *Fails at . . . _____.*
> *Looks bad at . . . _____.*
> *Is unpopular because . . . _____.*
> *I put that sin on the cross, and I receive your forgiveness.*

Things That Get Us Human Love May Not Be What God Wants for Us

The need for self-acceptance extends to another area of anxiety for many, and that is anxiety around achievement and success. Mary was a 32-year-old woman who began to experience anxiety related to her work. Over a number of sessions, we reviewed some of the dynamics of her workplace and how she experienced it. The workplace was highly competitive, and lists of employees with the highest metrics were posted weekly for everyone to see. Mary was very proud of being at or near the top regularly. However, the cost to her life was becoming untenable. She was getting calls at dinner and returning texts in bed. She did not have a moment's rest. Furthermore, when issues beyond her control caused her customers to get upset or her numbers to decline, her anxiety level would increase. Her need to perform at a certain level of excellence made it hard for her to accept any lesser outcome than what she envisioned.

Sometimes we become anxious regarding our need to succeed. "What if I don't get what I worked so hard for?" "What if I am not a success?" That can be especially hard when our sense of identity is being formed. In many cultures, a sense of identity is developed through achievement. When our achievement is threatened, so is our sense of self, our sense of who we are in society. For some people, the security in their sense of self is more fragile than for others, depending on the dynamics in their family of origin. If a family communicates love conditionally, expressing warmth, praise, and affection only when valued achievements are demonstrated and never otherwise, that lays the seeds for future problems.

For many people, their parents did the best they could. They wanted the best for their children and reinforced success in academia, sports, music, arts, or other realms because naturally they wanted their children to succeed. This is all well and good . . . unless the child only or mostly receives affirmation, love, attention, and acceptance when they perform or achieve in the area their parents are rewarding them for. This can lead to a lifetime of pursuing that particular kind of achievement in order to receive love and affirmation.

We all learn in some way or another to pursue the things that, when we were young, got us attention, got us admiration, or resulted in our receiving praise and warmth. We are conditioned to go after whatever we believe will get us love. The problem is that those things may not be what God intended for us. This self we develop is sometimes called the "false self." Jesus calls us to lay down anything that keeps us from him, and that applies to the false self as well.

Anxious Over Too Much to Do

There is always too much to do and too little time. There is also the reality that God invites us to do a limited set of things that fit within the boundaries he has placed in our lives. If we try to do more than what he is inviting us to, we run the risk of doing work for God out of our own strength, rather than by the power of the Spirit of God in us. When we start to "take over" from God, one of the side effects for many people is that they begin to experience anxiety. They begin to feel there is simply too much to do, they can't get it all done, and they are paralyzed and can't even start. This tends to perpetuate the anxiety because the less we do, the more our to-do list grows, and the feeling of being overwhelmed and anxious increases.

One irony here is that making a list of what to do is actually therapeutic. When we have our lists in our minds, we continue to worry that we might forget something. By putting it down on paper, it creates some distance and a sense of organization and control. The problem is that if the list is just too long for the time available, we begin to feel again the anxiety just described.

One solution I have found extremely helpful is to develop, and continually update, a Personal Rule of Life. It allows me to live intentionally and proactively, rather than reacting to the events of daily life. It helps me to maintain priorities that are important to me, and it helps me to stay within the margins of life God has ordained for me in a given season of my life. To understand more about how to create and use a Personal Rule of Life, we need to first look at God's intentions for our rhythms of life.

God created a natural world of daily, monthly, and seasonal rhythms. In the Old Testament, God prescribed rhythms of work and rest, festivals and worship, and so on. In addition to following the Old Testament rhythms, Jesus lived a life of intentional rhythms of prayer, work, and retreats. We need those rhythms in our lives as well, otherwise we risk losing much. A lack of healthy rhythms can create emotional, physical, and spiritual health problems for us. And, over time, this lack of healthy rhythms can decrease our effectiveness in every area of life.

Christian communities throughout history have tried to be intentional in planning their life together with rhythms of worship, meals, work, rest, and so on. Monastic communities developed or adapted what they called a "Rule of Life"—a simple set of commitments and rhythms that defined and shaped their life together. In many cases, they also added other intentional behaviors that they wanted to see in the community.

A Personal Rule of Life is much more individual. It is created by you and for you alone. It is not intended to oppress or restrict you. It is not a personal development plan for you to be more self-disciplined. It is meant rather to help you live intentionally in each of the major areas of your life, responding fully to the desires God has put in you. We are not of course talking about any desire we have, but only the desires God has put in us. A Rule could be as simple as one daily, one weekly, and one monthly practice. Living out these rhythms creates a healthy long-term approach to life that avoids burnout, builds joy, deepens life with God, and makes our life flow out of our connection with God rather than our own efforts.

If you find yourself struggling with anxiety over too much to do and not enough time, or if you feel a nudge from the Holy Spirit as you read this, you might consider trying it out. I have included a summary of how to create a Personal Rule of Life in Appendix A that you can follow to create your first draft.

My biggest challenge to living within the Rule I felt God invited me to was a semester in seminary where it just seemed impossible to do all the work within the time I had allocated in my Rule of Life. This was a dilemma. I was taking the classes in response to God's invitation to the best of my discernment, but the rhythm I felt invited to did not match.

In discernment situations where there seems to be a conflict between the ways God is calling us, it is good to get wise counsel. I sought wisdom from a wiser and older friend who had been helpful in the past. She helped me identify that I was keeping the Sabbath longer than I needed to. I used to consider Sunday evenings part of my Sabbath, but she pointed out that since I started Saturday evening, I could end Sunday evening. I did not feel God was asking me to do this for the long run, but for one semester it was OK, so I made the change for that semester. For my daily rhythms, however, if I had too much schoolwork to do, it still had to be done by eight in the evening, because then I needed one hour with my wife and then one hour for myself at the end of the day. I did not think I should give those up. But that meant that my pride might have to suffer if my grade dropped from an A to a B. On the other hand, if my grade dropped to a level I felt was unacceptable to God's call, then I would need to revisit that discernment. Living within the boundaries God gives us may require us to say no to some things we care about more than God does. I think, for example, God cared more about my marriage than an A on a paper.

Being Anxious about Getting Something God Doesn't Even Want for Me

This was a point of huge freedom for me. I had an undercurrent of anxiety about the type of status I wanted in life. The right kind of education, career, house, neighborhood, education for my children, were all high on my list of ambitions. Some of my goals I achieved, others I did not. But somewhere in my early forties, I began to feel very differently about all these things. I realized that some of these goals were not what God wanted for me after all, and a lightbulb came on in my brain. It made acceptance of the possible loss of desired status a lot easier, and my anxiety over it diminished. If Jesus didn't want something for me, then I sure shouldn't want it either, and if I had a hard time not wanting it, I needed to ask him for help to change that.

This crystalized for me as I read a book called *The Jesus I Never Knew* by one of my favorite authors, Philip Yancey. He writes that in his career as a journalist, he had the chance to interview many stars, including NFL football players, movie actors, music performers, best-selling authors, and so on. He also writes about people who have laid down their lives in radical ways for others, and in comparing the two he says:

> Our "idols" [the people the world sees as superstars] are as miserable a group of people as I have ever met. Most have troubled or broken marriages. Nearly all are incurably dependent on psychotherapy. In a heavy irony, these larger-than-life heroes seem tormented by self-doubt.
>
> I have also spent time with people I call "servants." Doctors and nurses who work among the ultimate outcasts, leprosy patients in rural India. A Princeton graduate who runs a hotel for the homeless in Chicago. Health workers who have left high-paying jobs to serve in a backwater town of Mississippi. . . .
>
> I was prepared to honor and admire these servants, to hold them up as inspiring examples. I was not prepared to envy them. Yet as I now reflect on the two groups side by side, stars and servants, the servants clearly emerge as the favored ones, the graced ones. Without question, I would rather spend time among the servants than among the stars: They possess qualities of depth and richness and even joy that I have not found elsewhere. . . . Somehow in the process of losing their lives they find them.[26]

In Laying Down Our Anxious, False Selves, We Gain Our True Selves

If our anxiety is a fear of failing to achieve a status that the world covets, maybe we can be off the hook. There is very good news in this. Philip Yancey based his observation on a saying of Jesus that is repeated in all four Gospels: "Those who try to gain their own life will lose it; but those who lose their life for my sake will gain it" (Matt. 10:39, GNT). What does it mean to lose our lives for Jesus' sake? Does it mean we all have to immediately sell everything and work among the poorest of the poor? Does it mean taking the greatest missionary risks that Jesus would take? Well, for some of us that might be God's call, but for each of us, God has a special path. As we follow Jesus step by step along the path he has for us, we begin to deny the parts of ourselves that aren't really true, that aren't life giving. We begin to shed things that the world tells us we should have, like pride and greed, like privilege and power, like watching out for "me first."

Much of the time the pursuit of these things leads to anxiety. As we let go of them, a new self emerges, a self that reflects more of the true self God intended for us to be all along. Indeed, a self that cares more about what God thinks than what others think, a new self of humility and kindness, of generosity and caring for others. This new self is also less anxious.

The amazing thing is that this new self is freer, truer, and more fully alive than the old one. It is just like Jesus describes it: if you lay your life down for him, you will save it. On the other hand, if you try to hang on to the old self, it is a road to emotional and spiritual death.

For some, the pattern of performing in order to receive love finds its way into their relationship with God. As a result, they may even go into ministry roles that have nothing to do with calling and more to do with trying to earn God's love. Of course, that's a fertile field for anxiety as well. If they don't succeed in ministry, all their growing up years have conditioned them to believe God will withhold his approval. Can you imagine how much anxiety that creates?

Getting back to my client Mary, as we worked together, she became aware of her father's very high standards of achievement for her, and her mother's disappointment that she did not choose a career with more prestige. Mary's childhood was full of social competitiveness. From camp, to church, to parents and grandparents, the message was consistent: performing better than others was the key to affirmation, love, respect, and so on. Mary was a fantastic athlete and a strong competitor, and this helped her to maintain a false self. Until we talked about it, she had simply not realized that this was not God's desire for her. As we worked on this, she began to see that her true self was a deeply caring, loyal, sensitive person, a deeply committed wife, mother, and follower of Jesus. All the other achievements became more and more secondary. She stopped obsessively checking the weekly chart of employee rankings. She began to reduce her work hours to a more balanced life. Mary is now less anxious and much more at peace with who God made her to be.

PART II

HOW TO PRAY THROUGH ROOT CAUSES OF ANXIETY

Chapter 6

Prayer for Trauma

JESUS KNOWS HOW TO HEAL TRAUMA. In John 21, he asked Peter a seemingly strange question: "Do you love me?" This had to hurt, because Peter knew there was a huge elephant in the room—namely, that he had not been able to stay with Jesus at his trial and had denied him. Can you imagine how awkward this felt to Peter? And then Jesus did another strange thing: he said it two more times. The chapter tells us Jesus' questions indeed hurt Peter's feelings. A less strange follow-up to each of the questions is Jesus asking Peter to feed his sheep. The content of what Jesus wanted Peter to know seems straightforward enough. He was essentially telling Peter: "I forgive you, I trust you, and I still want you to do the work of my Kingdom." If that was Jesus' message, then why say it in such a painful way? Why not just say: "Peter, I know you feel bad about what happened at the trial. I forgive you, but there's work to do in caring for my sheep, and I want you to do it." I believe the explanation is in a twenty-first-century understanding of how trauma is healed, a process called Memory Reconsolidation.

When someone experiences a traumatic event, their amygdala becomes highly activated. This in turn causes another brain structure, the hippocampus, to become highly activated. The hippocampus is involved in the storage of memories. The more highly activated it is, the stronger will be the memory that is stored and the harder it is to modify. One way to think about it is that it's like writing in a computer file a sentence in very large bold font, then changing the properties of that file from *read/write* to *read only*. That is why when someone talks about a traumatic memory, they often say, "I remember it as if it were yesterday." That's because they do indeed remember it very vividly; it's in big bold font. It also does not fade very much because the file is *read only*. It can't be overwritten.

Another complication is that the perception of the world someone has during the trauma also gets written down in big bold font, and, again, the file properties are changed to *read only*. For example, if a young woman experienced the trauma of rape as a teenager by a young man she was dating, she might develop a view of reality that says, "Men who are close to me can't be trusted and will hurt me when they get the chance." This is written in big bold font and is also stored in a file that is *read only*. She might later, in her twenties, come to realize that this is not true and start to date again and eventually become engaged to be married. Yet every time her fiancé is alone with her, she feels fear. She knows it's irrational. She tries to tell herself that this is silly and that he is a very different person than the teenager who raped her, but it does very little to calm the fear. Her anxiety rises because her thinking brain cannot overwrite that *read only* file.

This is where Memory Reconsolidation comes in. In their book *Unlocking the Emotional Brain*, Bruce Ecker, Robin Ticic, and Laurel Hulley describe the science and history of the development of this understanding of trauma. In simplest terms: In order to adequately heal the trauma, the traumatized person needs to experience at least some minimum activation of the amygdala again. This in turn will activate their hippocampus, creating conditions that turn the *read only* file into a *read/write* file. This is the point where it is very helpful for the person to experience a message of truth that overwrites the false message the trauma originally created. In therapy, the amygdala is not activated by new trauma but by a guided and safe recalling of the old memory.

One of my clients, who we will call Jane, was a 55-year-old woman who had been married for 30 years. She went through the very painful experience of discovering her husband had had an affair with a much younger woman. What's more, she'd had multiple experiences of betrayal in her childhood. This was excruciatingly painful for her. But she and her husband worked hard, each in their own therapy as well as in couples therapy, to find healing, growth, and transformation, all of which restored their marriage to a much better footing. However, one seemingly small issue remained distressing for her. During the affair, her husband had been texting his lover while in Jane's presence. Of course, she did not know this at the time but found out later. But even after therapy, every time he even looked at his phone, she felt panic rising within her.

In one of our sessions, we employed the Memory Reconsolidation approach. I asked Jane to describe what happened to her when her husband looked at his phone, and I asked her to allow herself to feel as much of the feeling as she could handle. She did so marvelously. At the height of her distress, when the conditions were ripe and the file was back in *read/write* mode, I asked her if her husband had changed. I asked her to tell me in some detail *how* he had changed since the affair and what new evidence of his complete faithfulness she had experienced recently. This had the effect of writing a new message that replaced the old one. We went through this a couple of more times during the session to reinforce the message. After just that one session, she was surprised to report that she was no longer affected when her husband looked at his phone.

Going back to the story of Peter, let's rewind and explore what happened to Peter during his traumatic experience. In Matthew 26, we find Peter trying to stay close to Jesus after his arrest by lurking around in the courtyard of the house where Jesus is being questioned by the high priest. Twice Peter is asked if he is with Jesus, and he says no. But he is very afraid; his amygdala is highly activated. Nonetheless, he manages to maintain enough determination to stand by Jesus without fleeing, even though the danger to himself increases as people seem to recognize him as one of Jesus' followers. However, the third time he is asked, he cannot hang on anymore. He curses and swears that he does not know Jesus and gets up and leaves. The chapter ends with him weeping bitterly.

Let's examine for a minute what Peter's hippocampus wrote in that *read-only* file in his brain. Of course, we can't know for sure, but we can take an educated guess that it was something like, "I don't have what it takes to follow Jesus like I thought I did." Another perception is, "I don't have what it takes to do what Jesus asked me to do for his Kingdom." Finally, I would guess there would be some serious doubt about Jesus even wanting him to do it, something like, "Jesus would not want me to do the work anyway, now that he knows my love for him is not as deep as it needs to be."

What Jesus does to heal Peter is a textbook example of Memory Reconsolidation. After Jesus' resurrection, in John 21, where we first started this discussion, he asks Peter, "Do you love me?" This has the direct effect of triggering Peter's amygdala as he remembers the event and how painful it was. Recalling the pain of that memory changes the *read only* file in Peter's brain into *read/write* mode. Jesus then goes ahead and gives him the new message that needs to replace the old one: "Feed my sheep." He replaces all the nagging doubts that have been plaguing Peter and that Peter cannot overwrite on his own. The message of "Jesus would not want me to do the work anyway, now that he knows my love for him is not as deep as it needs to be" is effectively replaced by "Jesus still knows I love him despite my weakness, and he still wants me to do the work." Now here's another fascinating part: Jesus does it three times, and in therapy, the process is repeated a few times depending on the circumstances and the methods used. After that point, we know Peter went on to have a highly effective and fruitful ministry.

Anxiety that is trauma-related needs more than exposure therapy. Exposure therapy could work, but it might be only temporary. Of course, experiencing some real relief when one is suffering is not without value. However, until the root memory is addressed, the anxiety might return. This is particularly true if avoidance patterns re-emerge or repetitive reassurance seeking comes back. In that case, the alarm center of the brain (the amygdala) is raising a false alarm not just because of its own misinterpretation or oversensitivity, but because there are *read only* files in other parts of the brain (likely the limbic system and right hemisphere) that have established a pattern of misinterpreting reality. Although exposure therapy is an important part of the answer, dealing with the root traumatic memory is also necessary. In doing so, these large bold font *read-only* files can be overwritten, and the amygdala will learn not to raise false alarms.

Generally, trauma therapy involves establishing a safe space for the client to relive the emotions associated with the memory and work through the grief of the events in safety, receiving comfort and truth in ways the client usually can't do on their own. Depending on the severity of the situation, I will once again repeat the recommendation I made in the Introduction: the prayer suggestions in this book do not replace working with a therapist. This is especially true when it comes to working with trauma.

What Constitutes Trauma?

Dr. Karl Lehman is a board-certified psychiatrist with twenty-five years and more than forty thousand hours of clinical experience. He has worked tenaciously throughout his career to integrate his personal Christian faith with medical science, modern mental healthcare, and his rigorous scientific training. He has especially worked to integrate faith-based emotional healing with insights provided by psychological and neurological research.[27]

He proposes a broad definition of trauma whereby the negative event need not be as massive as a war or hurricane. It can, in fact, be the result of what may seem to adults like a minor incident in a child's experience, but nevertheless one in which the child felt abandoned by a caregiver they expected would protect or rescue them—or at the very least show compassion and understanding.[28] Those memories, if not properly processed, can be triggered in adulthood by what to others may seem like a trivial event.

Dr. Lehman, in collaboration with Dr. Jim Wilder, has proposed a framework for how negative experiences can be processed in a healthy way in the brain. The framework has a total of five steps, two of which are of particular interest. The most crucial one for us to look at in this chapter is *attunement*. The second one we will look at is correctly interpreting the negative event, which we will discuss in the next chapter.

Dr. Lehman's functional definition of attunement is this:

> I am successfully *offering* **attunement** if I see you, hear you, correctly understand your internal experience, *join* you in the emotions you're experiencing, genuinely care about you, and am glad to be with you. And you are successfully *receiving* my **attunement** if you *feel* seen, heard, and understood, if you *feel* that I am *with* you in your experience, and if you *feel* that I care about you and that I am glad to be with you.[29]

For example, receiving attunement might look like a child who has fallen and been hurt on the playground and runs to a parent. The parent holds, comforts, and attends to the needs of the child. The child feels that his pain is understood and cared for, and that the parent wants to be with him. If this critical piece of the pain processing pathway is present, it is less likely that a negative event will turn into a trauma.

If, on the other hand in this hypothetical example, the parent is not available or capable of giving attunement, a small traumatic memory may develop. If the parent says instead "don't bother me, I told you not to play rough, you're always making a mess." If that happens, at a later time in life, the person may experience a "trigger."[30] They may experience a reversal in life that is not their fault, yet it triggers a feeling they can't shake that it's their fault somehow. Often, the emotions are strong but the anxiety itself doesn't make sense because we tend to look to the present for the causes of anxiety. And we may think we've found them. But often our attributions from the present are wrong.[31]

The entire package of emotions that come up when someone is triggered often give hints as to the origin because the person may sound or act like someone of a different age. The entire package from the time of the trauma is on display, including mannerisms and choice of words. In addition, the old lack of attunement also resurfaces. Dr. Lehman describes this loss of attunement as turning off our relational circuits. These neural pathways in our brains are engaged when we are in relationship with someone. It is very helpful to observe and begin to learn when we are triggered, when those circuits shut down, because it can help us act and pray in ways that will help to reduce our anxiety and other distressing emotions.

Following is a list of things to watch for in recognizing if our relational circuits are offline or not:[32]

- We do not feel connected to others, nor do we want to be.
- We do not see others as relational beings; we do not see their true hearts.

- We do not feel compassion for their thoughts and feelings.
- We are not glad to be with them.
- We are not able or willing to offer attunement.
- We tend to be rigid and unable to think outside the box.
- Small things will irritate us.
- We perceive others as adversaries instead of allies.
- We tend toward judging, interrogating, and fixing instead of joining with someone and understanding them.
- We tend to perceive the other person as a problem instead of an emotional resource.

Of course, it is possible for our relational circuits to be offline due to other distressing emotions that have to do with the present moment rather than a trigger from the past. When we recognize that our relational circuits are offline, however, is still worth noting whether we are triggered into that state or not. It's actually a significant part of our journey to maturity to hold distressing thoughts such as anger or fear while staying relational. When our relational circuits are offline, we will not make the best decisions, and we are likely to damage relationships. It is difficult for us to be at peace. We cannot deal with our present in an optimal way, nor can we address the wounds from the past in an effective manner. When our relational circuits are offline, getting them turned back on needs to be our first priority.[33]

The best antidote when we are in that situation is for us to *receive* attunement.[34] If someone can provide it for us, and we are able to receive it, the relational circuits can come back online. We can receive attunement from friends, family members, or in therapy. But we can also receive it from the Lord, though that generally takes some practice. We'll look at one way to do that in our discussion of Immanuel Approach prayer later in this chapter.

If attunement is not possible or available, engaging in expressions of appreciation until they lead us to a state of gratitude can help do the same thing.[35] Gratitude—as we saw in previous chapters—is helpful in calming down the amygdala, our brain's alarm system. It can also release oxytocin, a chemical in the brain that prepares us for bonding and attachment.[36] The Psalms tell us to deliberately appreciate the Lord's goodness, and they also model how to do it (see Psalm 7:17, Psalm 9:1-18, Psalm 18:1-50, Psalm 28:6-8, and Psalm 34:1-22, among many others).[37]

Just as attunement and gratitude can help get our relational circuits back online when we are triggered, they can also bring healing when applied to a traumatic memory. Often, attunement is the very emotional experience that needs to overwrite the *read only* file created during trauma, because the main damaging message was "I am alone in this," and receiving attunement is one part of changing that. Attunement and gratitude then are two critical components of the Immanuel Approach healing prayer model we are about to discuss.

Prayer for Healing from Trauma

Some individuals recover from trauma without therapy. Sometimes talking with empathetic family and friends immediately after a traumatic event is enough. At other times, therapy is needed. There are also several models of inner healing prayer that have been developed in various Christian traditions. Reviewing all of them is beyond the scope of this book, and almost all of them require the assistance of someone trained to pray using that particular model. The Immanuel Approach, pioneered by Karl Lehman, is designed to be facilitated by a trained person, and Dr. Lehman cautions against trying it on your own first.[38] However, after some experience with a trained facilitator (some people need less assistance, some more), individuals may be able to effectively practice it on their own.

Dr. Lehman says the chances of a positive experience are greatly increased with a facilitator, partly due to the help they can offer with troubleshooting, providing more faith, helping you keep your experiences in focus, and getting you unstuck if you stumble on a particularly difficult traumatic memory. If any of these negative consequences happen in personal practice first, the likelihood of giving up on Immanuel Prayer increases.

Healing from trauma, as discussed earlier, usually occurs when the traumatized person recalls the experience and the emotions associated with the trauma in the presence of a caring person, who can provide attunement and ideally help them with experiencing an opposite message to the one that was created during the trauma. In the case of Immanuel Prayer, we go to Jesus directly for that attunement and let him guide the re-writing. A fuller understanding of the approach can be found at www.immanuelapproach.com, but here is a brief outline of what usually happens.

1. Create the conditions for healing.

We begin by remembering a time in our relationship with God for which we are deeply grateful, a time when we sensed God's presence and his care for us. It can be a time of answered prayer, a time of a special encounter with the Lord, or any situation where we felt very positive in our relationship with God. After we dwell on that memory, we can pray that God would help us transition from remembering him being with us to perceiving him with us as a living presence.

Relationships are memory maps. That is, the relationship is carried by memories. For instance, without memories you can't have much of a relationship. But when you activate a memory of a relationship in your brain, you strengthen the relationship. When we think about, talk about, and recall previous memories of connecting with God, we actually strengthen our relationship with him neurologically and prepare our brain to do it again in the present, especially if we express our gratitude to him for that situation. Dr. Lehman explains that this turns on our personal awareness of God's presence in the present.

This perception of his presence is both experiential and theological. The latter is the basis for the name Immanuel, the awareness of "God with us."

2. Recall the traumatic event and feelings (or ask Jesus what he wants to address).

Only when we have bathed ourselves in gratitude to God for his presence and care in that earlier positive situation are we ready for the next step. Here we have a choice: we can ask Jesus to help us deal with a particular memory, or we can ask him to take us where he wants. If we choose to let him drive, we wait for him to bring a memory to us of his choosing. If we are more intentional and want to invite him into a particular memory, we can pray for that instead.

If the memory is upsetting, we open our minds to recall the circumstances and emotions associated with the trauma or distressful situation for which we need healing. We go back to the memory of that trauma and visualize and recall what happened and how it made us feel. This may be very unsettling, causing grief, pain, fear, and a sense of abandonment and confusion. Tears and other physical responses may erupt. (Trauma affects and is "remembered" in the whole body, not just the brain.) But a reaction, up to a certain point, is okay, as long as we are able to stay in that safe place with the Lord Jesus, whose presence we affirmed just a few minutes before. But we need to sit with our feelings long enough until we have words to describe them. If the feelings are too intense, the facilitator can move us on to Step 5 and go to our safety net. Also, if the facilitator notices that we are not able to continue experiencing the Lord's presence from the previous step in our distress, then they will also employ the safety net and move on to Step 5.

3. *Bring our pain to the Lord Jesus.*

In this whole process, Jesus is our therapist, so now is the time to actually tell him about the event, verbally describing what happened and naming the negative feelings it created. If you are tempted to think your feelings don't matter to God, remember that feelings are important to God and expressing them to him has been part of Christian tradition not only in the Psalms, but also in hymns like this one:

> *I must tell Jesus all of my trials;*
> *I cannot bear these burdens alone;*
> *In my distress He kindly will help me;*
> *He ever loves and cares for His own.*

I must tell Jesus all of my troubles;
He is a kind, compassionate Friend;
If I but ask Him, He will deliver,
And in my griefs with me He will blend.[39]

4. Receive Jesus' comfort.

Be bold enough to receive in your mind and heart what Jesus says back to you in response to bringing your trauma to him. Jesus' response may come in actual words impressed on your consciousness, or you may receive a feeling to which you need to put words. The facilitator might ask you what you heard Jesus saying to you. Verbalize back to Jesus directly what he said to you by thanking him out loud for what he's said: "Thank you, Jesus for understanding . . ." "Thank you for telling me . . ." "Thank you for showing me . . ." "Thank you for being there when I felt so alone." Actually, talking to Jesus in some similar way will help solidify and verify the healing he is providing. It is amazing to me how Jesus will provide the exact experience that the person needs to overwrite those *read only* files.

At this point, the most common obstacle is to feel we are putting words in Jesus' mouth. This is of course a very legitimate concern, but fortunately one we can address. Like other ways of hearing from God subjectively, we need to apply some filters. We need to "test the spirits" as 1 John 4:1 encourages us to. First, we need to know that we filter everything we hear through our own personhood, and God knows that. To an extent, we do put words in Jesus' mouth, but our desire is that those words reflect his thoughts.

Second, we need to treat what we hear with all the accepted rules of discernment that Christian tradition offers, as I will discuss in Chapter 8. Nonetheless, it bears repeating. We reject thoughts that are not in line with Scripture and what it teaches us about the character of Jesus. If we have any doubts, we can express this to a person whose wise counsel we respect and if they reject it, we need to doubt it as well. If the result is not more peace and more love and more fruits of the Spirit (Galatians 5:22-23) and does not align with attitudes from the Sermon on the Mount (Matthew 5–7), then that is also cause to reject it. It is important to accept that we can make mistakes in hearing from Jesus just as we might hear wrongly from other people, and yet this does not stop us from interacting with them.[40] Finally, I asked Dr. Lehman his opinion on this, and he said quite simply, "If there is healing that stays, we know it's from Jesus."

5. A safety net.

Several things might interfere with making it all the way through to full healing at this point. You may not have enough time or may be interrupted somehow. You may experience some relief but sense there is more healing to come. These conditions are understandable and do not represent failure. Instead, if you have even a few minutes, use this safety net to come up out of the review of your trauma. Return to the first step and recall and thank God for the good situation you earlier experienced. This will make it easier to return to the process again in the future. But when you do, begin with setting the conditions for healing by starting with Step 1.[41]

Healing from trauma doesn't mean future memories of the incident won't bring tears. By definition, a trauma is a sad event or circumstance that shouldn't have happened to anyone. If healing has taken place, that sadness is more like the empathy we'd feel in hearing of it happening to anyone. But if healing has happened, it won't continue to debilitate you or trigger unreasonable responses.

My Experience Applying the Immanuel Approach

While the science behind these steps is complicated and conditions for healing to take place are challenging from a human perspective, Dr. Lehman says, "If we are able to perceive the Lord's presence, establish a connection with him, and receive adequate assistance from him, this potentially complicated process can become very simple."[42]

In my first experience with Immanuel Prayer, the model seemed to work beautifully. I was at an introductory training event for Immanuel Prayer. The person facilitating for me and I were both trying this for the first time. Unknowingly, I went to a memory that was both distressing and positive at the same time. I later learned that was not ideal, but, hey, it was my first time. What I remembered was a situation where one of my children was sick. He was a toddler at the time and had some sort of upper respiratory infection. His sleep was disturbed, and he kept coughing and tossing and turning. I remembered kneeling by the bed and praying. I was weary from being so anxious for my kids' health, and I asked God an immature and tired question: Would he show me that he cared for my family? As I continued to pray by the bedside, my child's breathing improved, and he slept more peacefully. Years later in the Immanuel Prayer exercise, I remembered this positive experience of God answering my prayer, and I tried to perceive Jesus' presence in the situation. In my mind, I expected to see him putting his hand on the baby's head and praying for him. Instead, I perceived Jesus kneeling beside me, putting his hand on *my* shoulder, and praying for *me*!

Even though this may seem a minor event, when my children were young, their health had always been a major source of anxiety for me, as I described earlier. My first attempt at Immanuel Prayer allowed me to experience Jesus' attunement in this memory. It healed me of something I was not even aware of. I had judged myself for all these worries and not trusting God, and felt God was far from me in it. Experiencing Jesus' compassion for me in my worry healed this.

Often, the negative experiences that Jesus chooses to go after are situations where we did not get the things we needed, whether love, attention, nurture, or so on. Even though we don't normally think of those as traumatic events, they create memories that later get "triggered" in similar ways.

In one situation I was facilitating Immanuel Prayer with someone who had suffered both trauma and depression. She was courageously seeking treatment and progressing. However, the depression seemed to linger, and the sense of anger at God for being absent from her suffering was palpable.

As we worked through the steps of the Immanuel Prayer, Jesus brought to mind a memory of her eighth birthday. Her cake was on the counter. She stayed at the dinner table for what seemed like a very long time waiting for her father to come home from work and celebrate her birthday and have cake. She eventually gave up. He seldom came home for dinner. In the prayer time, Jesus brought the cake to her and celebrated with her. He gave her a special gift. When I asked her what it was, she said she did not know exactly, except she knew how it made her feel. It was the type of gift that is so thoughtful and shows that you know the person deeply. She really needed this because she did not feel known by her father.

Then the scene shifted, and she was running through the woods joyfully, and Jesus was running with her. This was also significant, she told me, because in real life she always had to tag along to be with her dad, with whatever he was doing. He never went where she wanted to go. The specificity with which Jesus met her deep needs is remarkable to say the least.

Our Personal Time of Prayer, Immanuel Lifestyle

Even beyond healing from debilitating traumas, you will notice that the steps Dr. Lehman has outlined provide an ideal pattern for communicating with God on a daily basis. Life always includes bumps and bruises as we face disappointments, failures, slights from friends, and actual injustices. Usually, we simply roll with the punches and get over those things without lasting repercussions to ourselves or others. However, how much better to reset our emotional equilibrium at least daily. And the steps of the Immanuel Prayer work as well for small things alone as for large traumas we work through with someone else. Dr. Lehman calls this the Immanuel Lifestyle, wherein applying these steps can help us to remove obstacles that keep us from intimacy with Jesus on a regular basis.

One question I get asked often is whether we can experience attunement directly from the Lord in our prayer time. There is an exercise for this developed by Dr. E. James Wilder and his colleagues that they describe in their book *Joyful Journey: Listening to Immanuel*. We can do the exercise as follows:

Step 1—I see you. Start by writing a letter from God to you where he begins by saying, "I see you . . ." and then fill in the blank. For example, "I see you, Joanne, on your deck drinking your coffee in your bright blue and white dress." Then go to observations God would make about your internal state, such as, "I can see the tension in your shoulders" or "I can see you are anxious to the point that your mouth feels dry."

Step 2—I hear you. Write down what God hears you thinking, like, "I hear you saying you wish you had never taken on this project." Then move to the thoughts beneath those words, like, "I hear the desperation you feel."

Step 3—I can understand how big (hard) this is for you. This is a chance to let ourselves feel God's validation for how we are feeling about the scale of the issue: "I understand how deeply disturbing this is to you."

Step 4—I am near you and glad to be with you and treat your weaknesses tenderly. This step is about allowing ourselves to feel God's closeness, his kindness and tenderness toward us. It can sound something like, "I am so glad to have this time with you, my daughter. I am always wanting to be with you and close to you in your pain."

Step 5—I can do something about what you are going through. In this step, God gives us guidance and support. It may sound like, "I will not forget you; don't forget that your name is carved on the palm of my hand."

Step 6—Read it out loud. It is also helpful, after writing the letter, to read it out loud to God.[43]

Chapter 7

Psalms for Healing the Soul

INHERITED A COPY OF *The Agpeya* FROM MY DAD—a book from the Egyptian Coptic Church that traces its roots to the author of the Gospel of Mark. The Coptic Church in Egypt was on the forefront of monastic movements in the early years of Christianity, and that tradition has continued until the present day, where it plays a significant role in the life of this church.

The Agpeya contains all the prayers the monks pray at different hours of the day. Almost all high church traditions have some combination of prayers that are said at set times of the day. It is a continuation, with adaptations, of the Jewish prayer traditions as practiced by Jesus and his contemporaries. Christian adaptations vary from one tradition to another, but they almost always involve praying the Psalms along with other readings and prayers, including the Lord's Prayer.[44]

The preface to *The Agpeya* says the Coptic church believes the Psalms bring healing to our souls. This is not just an ancient view. Scot McKnight, a New Testament theologian, writes: "Spiritual health begins to arrive at our door when we level with God the way the Psalms do."[45]

The psychiatrist Curt Thompson, in his book *Anatomy of the Soul*, says that poetry accesses the right side of our brain by activating the sense of rhythm. It also stimulates buried emotional states and layers of memory and serves as a way to connect the right brain with the left brain because it uses the language centers on the left side.[46] This creates a sense of integration of many layers of our brain. It counteracts our brain's unfortunate tendency to disconnect from its various parts and helps us to regain a more connected mind, which Thompson describes as the mind of Christ.[47] This is because a more interconnected mind is healthier, and Jesus—it is safe to say—had the healthiest mind of all!

Walter Brueggemann, a contemporary Old Testament theologian, says in his book *Spirituality of the Psalms* that "these Psalms make the important connection: everything must be brought to speech, and everything brought to speech must be addressed to God, who is the final reference for all of life."[48]

Further on, he says:

> What we do know, both from the structure of the text and our own experience, is that grievance addressed to an authorized partner does free us. That is the insight behind Freud's theory of talk-therapy, that we do not move beyond the repressed memory unless we speak it out loud to one with authority who hears. In our culture we have understood that in terms of one-on-one therapy. We still have to learn that this is true socially and liturgically. These psalms provide important materials for that learning.[49]

It's important to process with God what we are feeling. This deepens our friendship and intimacy with God. It also brings healing. It brings a sense of being heard by God, that somehow God feels our feelings. This creates a sense of secure attachment[50] that we will discuss further in Chapter 10.

Brueggemann divides the Psalms into three types: Psalms of Orientation, Psalms of Disorientation, and Psalms of Reorientation. Psalms of Orientation affirm the rightness of things and of God. Early on in my faith journey, I bought into the idea that God wanted everything to be nice and easy for me, and if I stayed clear of sin and prayed hard enough, he would help to ensure that. Unfortunately, many of our churches today promote that idea. We want to see Jesus only as victor, not as the suffering servant. The very first Psalm falls into this category:

> *Blessed is the one*
>> *who does not walk in step with the wicked*
> *or stand in the way that sinners take*
>> *or sit in the company of mockers,*
> *but whose delight is in the law of the* LORD,
>> *and who meditates on his law day and night.*
> *That person is like a tree planted by streams of water,*
>> *which yields its fruit in season*
> *and whose leaf does not wither —*
>> *whatever they do prospers.*
>
> *Not so the wicked!*
>> *They are like chaff*
>> *that the wind blows away.*
> *Therefore the wicked will not stand in the judgment,*
>> *nor sinners in the assembly of the righteous.*
>
> *For the* LORD *watches over the way of the righteous,*
>> *but the way of the wicked leads to destruction.*

Psalms of Disorientation, the second type of Psalms, are the exact opposite. They are about a world that does not make sense, a world where the unjust are rewarded and the just suffer, where there is doubt, fear, loneliness, and so on. These are Psalms where King David is bewildered by what is happening to him. He spent eight years on the run for his life when he was innocent. He was betrayed by close friends. In the middle of all of this messiness, David writes these Psalms of Disorientation, pouring his heart out to God about the nightmare that his life has become. Some of these Psalms are so honest, they are hard to hear. Consider Psalm 88:13-18:

> But I cry to you for help, LORD;
> in the morning my prayer comes before you.
> Why, LORD, do you reject me
> and hide your face from me?
>
> From my youth I have suffered and been close to death;
> I have borne your terrors and am in despair.
> Your wrath has swept over me;
> your terrors have destroyed me.
> All day long they surround me like a flood;
> they have completely engulfed me.
> You have taken from me friend and neighbor —
> darkness is my closest friend.

In the middle of all that darkness, these Psalms wonder where God is. They express doubt, fear, pain, and loneliness. They speak of betrayal and anguish. We would rather not deal with those feelings. These are the kinds of things we don't talk about in polite company. Perhaps we discuss them with our therapist, or in a Twelve Step meeting, but sometimes we hesitate to bring them to God. Furthermore, for those individuals who grew up in homes where feelings like that were never allowed to be spoken, it's very hard to admit them to themselves, let alone to God.

Finally, the third type of Psalm are the Psalms of Reorientation, which help us get back on track with God. Our picture of God expands to include our hard experiences, where our faith has grown to include faith in the middle of suffering. A good example is from Psalm 73:21-26.

> *When my heart was grieved*
> *and my spirit embittered,*
> *I was senseless and ignorant;*
> *I was a brute beast before you.*
>
> *Yet I am always with you;*
> *you hold me by my right hand.*
> *You guide me with your counsel,*
> *and afterward you will take me into glory.*
> *Whom have I in heaven but you?*
> *And earth has nothing I desire besides you.*
> *My flesh and my heart may fail,*
> *but God is the strength of my heart*
> *and my portion forever.*

Post-Traumatic Growth

This concept of orientation, disorientation, and reorientation is often what happens as we struggle with trauma. Research I encountered during my counseling studies examined incidents in which people actually experienced growth after trauma, known as Post-Traumatic Growth.

Most people have heard of PTSD, Post-Traumatic Stress Disorder, where following an experience of trauma, symptoms show up such as flashbacks, nightmares, distress reactions to things that remind them of the trauma, and so on. . . . But new research shows that does not have to be the only outcome from trauma. Studies indicate that after serious trauma occurs, there are four possible outcomes.[51]

The first possibility is that the person is affected negatively in an ongoing way, developing PTSD, which puts them below the baseline of mental health they were at before the trauma.

Second, the person might recover back to their previous baseline. This happens usually with some therapy. Others—depending on their genetics, life story, support system, and the severity of the trauma—recover to their baseline without therapy.

The third possibility is the most interesting. After going through a trauma and following recovery from that trauma, they end up at a higher level of functioning than their previous baseline. They seem to develop a greater sense of purpose, a deeper relationship with God, a greater love for others, and a greater appreciation for life. This is what's called PTG, Post Traumatic Growth.

But there is a fourth possibility. After the person recovers and even experiences Post Traumatic Growth, they may still experience symptoms of PTSD. The two conditions are not mutually exclusive. Perhaps the best phrase that illustrates this is the title of Henri Nouwen's book *The Wounded Healer*. The question clinicians ask, of course, is, How do we get to option three, where the person experiences healing and Post Traumatic Growth without continuing the PTSD?

Parallels to What the Psalms Describe

The Psalms indicate that when trauma happens, our disorientation and pain can be so deep we feel lost. Consequently, we may or may not experience God in the midst of that darkness. Yet the Psalms tell us that ultimately, as we continue to be faithful to bring our feelings to God, we will experience a deeper shift. This reorientation of our worldview is something similar to Post Traumatic Growth. It doesn't deny the pain, but it clings to the confidence that ultimately good will come. Psalm 30:5 affirms: "Weeping may stay for the night, but rejoicing comes in the morning." Dr. Wilder puts it this way:

> When pain has been fully processed, the experience usually produces wisdom. What caused us pain was not always a good thing, but full resolution brings good from everything. This is redemption. If we allow God to take us through a proper pain-processing sequence, we develop deeper compassion and empathy. Moreover, those who courageously allow this process to bear fruit ultimately find they love God and others more deeply.[52]

In this process, our worldview shifts from not knowing how God allows suffering to being able to embrace it. Recognizing that God is in the middle of it *with* us transforms us, making us people who are better and more able to love effectively than before. We become people who increasingly share God's heart for life and for others, which creates a more resilient spiritual perspective and emotional reality.

As I mentioned earlier, many church traditions include Psalms as part of set daily prayer times. Some devotional guides also include a reading from the Psalms for each day. It is a suggestion I will include as well: make reading a Psalm or portion of a Psalm part of your daily time with God, maybe listening to it in song format. See if it is life-giving to you.

Prayers That Hinder versus Prayers That Help

Research into PTG has primarily focused on a practice called "positive rumination." It attempts to process and make sense of a traumatic experience without it becoming an intrusive and unwanted thought. Reviewing our pain with God is just such a positive rumination.

One less-researched aspect of what helps promote PTG is the impact of various types of prayer. One researcher did find, however, that superficial prayers such as, "God, please take this away," over and over again, are ineffective in producing PTG. Such prayers are not theologically wrong; they're just the first step, not the whole picture.

But the same research also found that prayers focusing on asking God for calm and acceptance correlated more closely with PTG than simply asking him to rescue us and help us avoid pain.[53] This makes sense not only because of the benefits of acceptance we described in Chapter 2 but also because as God answers prayers for calm and acceptance, he creates the space we need to process our trauma with someone else and with him. It effectively allows us space to work out our "positive rumination" with him in prayer. This is especially relevant when the anxiety of the present moment itself is what we need to process with God, instead of the original trauma. If an original trauma caused ongoing anxiety about the world being unsafe, processing our *feelings* about the world being unsafe and how that fits in with our relationship with God is critical.

This kind of positive rumination with God will bring about growth in our relationship with him. It will help us also to reinterpret a negative event that turned into a trauma. As we've seen earlier, misguided interpretations of reality as a result of trauma are common, so getting that corrected is an important part of our healing and relationship with God.

Chapter 8

Fear of Missing God's Will

ONE CAUSE OF ANXIETY I've found to be almost universal among serious Christians is a spectrum of anxieties related to discernment. There are two common varieties of this anxiety. The first is a fear of "missing God's will" in a life-direction decision. The second involves having to make an immediate practical decision where the stakes are high—for example, two doctors with different opinions on whether a potentially life-saving surgery is needed. Fortunately, developing a spiritually healthy approach to discernment helps in both situations.

Basics of Discernment

The basics of Christian discernment emphasized in most Christian traditions is to first ask whether the decision involves a potential violation of what the Bible says. At one point in my career in science and technology, my skills were in enough demand that I got calls from recruiters offering various opportunities. One prospect at first seemed quite interesting, and as the recruiter talked, I began considering the possibility. Then he said it was for a telephone service that sold, among other things, phone sex. That clearly did not align with what the Scriptures teach about sex, so the decision was a very clear no. In some Christian traditions, the church's interpretation of the Scriptures is also emphasized, and if that's the tradition you belong to, respecting church teachings is an important part of the discernment process as well.

The second thing is to invite input from wise people who are mature in their relationship with God. Many years ago, I had a friend leading a ministry where my wife was serving. We thought he was clearly wrong about an issue. I thought I should be open with him about my concerns, as Matthew 18 teaches. But I first sought wise counsel because I knew it was a sensitive issue for his ministry and our relationship. The first two people I consulted said no, it was his ministry, this was well within his purview, and my questioning him might seem like unfair second guessing or that I was biased toward my wife's viewpoint. I was still not convinced, so I asked one more person, but he said the same thing. Finally, I decided I must be missing something and listened to everyone's wise counsel. In retrospect, I can see they were right.

The third way we can tell what God wants is to notice whether we have an internal conviction of whether something is right, even if sometimes our feelings have not caught up with our convictions. A friend of mine was unhappy in her work and felt that God was leading her to a life of ministry. She looked at multiple options, but felt reluctant for various reasons, including cost, not wanting to move to another state, and so on. Then she ran across a highly specific seminary program that she just knew was what God had for her. The cost and the relocation no longer felt like obstacles. She simply knew this was where God was calling her. Sometimes it's that simple. When all three of the above criteria align, we can experience a measure of confidence that at least we are not actively going *against* God's will.

Often if a decision passes the first three tests, but we still feel some hesitation, it may be because we are facing a choice between two goods.[54] That does not automatically mean God does not have a preference. To find out, some additional work in prayer may be necessary. Yet, we can experience a reduction in anxiety by knowing we are not stepping away from God.

From Analysis to Discernment

Many years ago, a popular movement made the letters WWJD ubiquitous. They stood for *What Would Jesus Do?* The idea was to ask ourselves that question at every turn and imitate him. Not a bad first step. In fact, it is an excellent first step. But it is *only* a first step. Asking ourselves that question is where we begin discernment, but in essence it is an analysis of what we *think* God wants. It is not *asking* God what he wants, which is what discernment really is about.

I remember sitting in my first small group Bible study in college. It was in a friend's dorm room, and someone had brought chocolate chip cookies she had baked. It was very welcoming.

The topic of discussion that day was how God spoke to Abraham and told him he would bless him and so on. As the discussion proceeded, I shared something I was very hung up on (though no one else in the room seemed to be bothered by it). It was whether God would actually speak to someone that clearly. In the Bible story it sounded like God was on the other end of a phone call, and I was not shy to challenge the group over that understanding.

What the small group leader said in response was very wise. He said something like, "Isn't it our challenge, though, to get to know God as well as Abraham did, so we can hear him that clearly?" Today I would add a qualifier: not only do we need to know God, but we also need to get familiar with his voice. And our ability to hear God is often sharpened best in prayer.[55]

If we want to go beyond analyzing God's will to discerning it, prayer is what makes that possible.[56] Henri Nouwen says that "the way of discernment begins with prayer."[57] If we are trying to sense which way God is leading us, it makes sense that we do that in prayer. When we are faced with a decision, our history with God in prayer and discernment will come in handy as we come to him again. If we don't have that kind of history, it makes sense to begin to build it now. As a starting point, here are some ideas of what to ask God for. You can ask:

- For wisdom and discernment in the matter at hand.
- To increase your conviction of his will.
- To increase your desire for what he wants and decrease it for what he does not want.
- To guide your thoughts and feelings about the matter.
- To speak through the wise counsel of others as described above.
- To close the wrong doors and open the right doors and lead you through them.

More Ways to Practice Discernment

For myself, after a few days of praying some combination of the above list, I usually begin to sense a clearer leading internally as to which decision God is guiding me toward. When that doesn't happen, it's sometimes worth trying a couple of additional exercises.

Emptying yourself

David Benner is a psychiatrist and a spiritual director who wrote a book about discerning God's will. He said the real question is about truly wanting what God wants. He says, "The focus on God's will is thus misplaced—limited to points of major decisions. We fail to recognize that our problem is not so much knowing God's way as being utterly convinced that choosing God is choosing life."[58]

One series of steps for discernment comes from the Ignatian tradition of the Jesuits. Ignatius of Loyola taught that there are three stages we can be at in discernment. He called them "times."[59] Before we even start the process that he taught, he says that one of the first things to do is to pray for a sense of "indifference," caring only about God's desire in a situation. Ignatius then describes the effort as a grace that God gives us, not something we strive toward. It is wise then to begin by asking God for indifference in the face of a decision.[60]

In the "First Time" there is no question about what to do. We just know. This is similar to the story I told above about my friend knowing immediately that her next step was to go to seminary and which seminary program in particular. She just knew. It can be, and it often is, that straightforward for many decisions.

When we don't have that immediate knowing, we could be in the "Second Time." In this stage, we may not know immediately, but as we talk about it and pray about it, it becomes gradually clearer. Ignatius then says we should pay attention to which choice brings us a sense of "consolation" versus "desolation."

His definition of consolation revolves around a sense of rightness, of peace and of joy.[61] He says it is "every increase in hope, faith, and charity, and every interior joy which calls and attracts one toward heavenly things and to the salvation of one's soul, by bringing it tranquility and peace in its Creator and Lord."[62] As for desolation, he defines it as an increase in agitation, restlessness, or in Ignatius's words, feeling "listless, tepid, and unhappy."[63] He says it is "obtuseness of soul, turmoil within it, an impulsive motion toward low and earthly things, or disquiet from various agitations and temptations. These move one toward lack of faith and leave one without hope and without love."[64]

A regular rhythm of paying attention to experiences of consolation and desolation in our lives causes our discernment to sharpen significantly. This regular rhythm is called the Examen. Ignatius recommended his followers practice it three times a day. Mother Theresa used to do it twice a day. Many others, myself included, find it is even helpful to do it once a day at the beginning of our prayer time. There are various ways of performing the Examen. Some are more elaborate and formal than others.

The Examen has five steps. Before we start, though, we ask for God's grace to guide us, so really, it's six steps:

1. Ask God for his grace to guide us.
2. Begin by giving thanks for all the blessings of the previous day.

3. Ask God for grace to notice and repent of any sin of the previous day.
4. Review your day and identify periods of consolation and desolation. This step is the essence of the exercise.
5. Ask for forgiveness of any sins God may have brought to mind.
6. Ask for God's grace for the coming day.

I personally choose a more direct summarized approach that I've adapted. I simply review my last day with God, and I notice with him where I felt consolation and give him thanks. I also notice where I felt desolation, and if there is sin involved, I repent of it and receive his forgiveness. If not, I try to look for what is keeping me from God in that situation and pray accordingly for that to lift.

Doing this exercise regularly makes us better and better at discerning God's movement in our lives. After doing this exercise for months or years, when we are faced with a larger decision, we are more comfortable in asking ourselves which decision feels like it leads to more consolation or desolation. Clearly, the direction God is inviting us toward should feel a greater sense of consolation.

Another way I learned to do the Examen was taught to me by a Jesuit, Fr. Matt Linn, at an Ignatian retreat where he was my spiritual director. Fr. Linn was one of the earliest authors on prayer healing ministry. His recommendation is to begin by remembering the part of the day where we felt most loved or able to most love someone else. Press into the memory until the feeling returns. Stay with that feeling for a while. Then we go to the parts of the day that were more difficult, where we did not feel loved or were not able to love others. We perceive Jesus holding us as we review those memories and the feelings they created in us. We then return to the first memory of loving or being loved, and we close with that. Fr. Linn suggests we do this before sleeping, so that through the night, our brain is settled on the healing power of love.

When it comes time to make a decision and we start talking and praying about it, when it feels like we may be sensing a nudge in one direction, it is good to check whether that direction feels like consolation or desolation to us. Recognizing which it is will be much easier if we have had the benefit of practicing the Examen for some time.

Trying it on

Another exercise that can be helpful in the "Second Time" is to imagine making a choice and living with it for a while. Then pretend you made the opposite decision and live with that for a while.[65] By doing this, some things may come to light around a particular direction you hadn't anticipated. After living with each decision for a few days, you can evaluate which imagined direction brought you a greater sense of consolation.

Making two lists

At this point, if we still don't have clarity, we are most likely in the "Third Time." If we are in this stage, Ignatius suggests a very commonsense exercise of creating lists of pros and cons, but he adds some key elements to give it a whole new dimension. He suggests these steps.

1. Begin by praying for indifference.
2. In prayer, review the decision you need to make.
3. Ask yourself what your ultimate goal is. For Ignatius it was the desire to please God.

4. Pray that God would move your heart in the direction of the option he wants.

5. Make the list of pros and cons, once for each of the two options you are considering. (You can make the list as many times as you have options to decide between.)

6. Pray about the lists. I personally take time to pray through each of the pros and cons. Once I'm done, I add another twist: I redo the lists and see what has shifted. Whether you do the lists once or twice, after praying through it you will likely start to have a sense of leading in one direction or the other.

7. Ask for confirmation from God about the decision. This may be an external event, or it may be the sense of consolation.

8. Run the decision by people of wise counsel to get final confirmation.[66]

Objectivity

If the above exercises are not enough and there is still anxiety around the decision, there are a few more exercises we can try. One simple exercise is to imagine an anonymous person you do not know asking you for advice on the same decision you need to make. What would you tell them?

The second exercise is a bit macabre, but it is valuable. Think of yourself at the end of your life: Which decision would you look back and wish you had made? Similarly, think of yourself before God after you die: Which choice would you rather present to God? A less forward-looking view of the same exercise would be to ask yourself what your "best self" would do. If you were more fully the person you want to be, which choice would you make?[67]

One of the biggest decisions I made in my life in recent years was to make a final move away from a corporate career, while doing counseling and ministry part time, to full-time counseling and ministry. This was not a minor easy decision. I would be giving up a lot of financial security. I also knew that ministry is not always easy and has its own set of challenges. Although it was a big decision, it was not very difficult.

When I was in the corporate world full time, the work I did part time in counseling and spiritual direction, teaching and mentoring, always felt like consolation. Previously, when I had thought of doing ministry full time, at first I did not feel consolation. Some years later, however, it seemed that God's time had come, and I felt significant consolation. Even so, it was not without some trepidation around finances that I faced the decision. However, the final two exercises made it clear: if I imagined myself at the end of my life wondering which decision I should have made, the answer was very clear. And when I felt connected with God's purpose for my life, the decision, again, was very clear. Finally, when I sought confirmation from wise men and women with whom I met regularly for peer supervision in spiritual direction, their support for my decision was also clear.

It was a yes!

PART III

DEVELOPING A STRONGER SPIRITUAL IMMUNE SYSTEM

Chapter 9

Overcoming Hindrances to Prayer

THERE ARE MULTIPLE WAYS OF GROWING SPIRITUALLY and developing greater resilience in the face of anxiety. I believe one of the most effective is personal prayer. We will explore in the rest of this book how growth in prayer can increase our ability to deal with anxiety. One of the first things we need to do is deal with some common problems people face in growing in their prayer lives.

Over my years of mentoring people in prayer, culminating in my doctoral work on the topic, I have made many suggestions that are probably commonly known, and we just need to remind ourselves of them now and then. But some suggestions seem genuinely surprising and helpful to people. Hopefully, they will prove useful to you in growing a deeper relationship with God, even in the face of anxiety.

Confusing Things

Some people, steeped in Christian traditions that heavily emphasize Scripture, conclude that Scripture reading is so paramount, it displaces prayer. There are ways to engage with Scripture prayerfully (see Chapter 11), but as critical as reading and knowing Scripture is, prayer is also critical to our spiritual lives. We cannot have a healthy spirituality with just Scripture and no prayer, nor is the reverse healthy either. Jesus did both, and we are called to do both. We must not do one at the expense of the other.

A second area of confusion is the idea that talking with God throughout the day is a substitute for setting aside a specific time dedicated to prayer. One of the most common things I hear is, "I pray all the time; I don't need to set aside a time for prayer." While this is a good practice to cultivate, it should not take the place of dedicated time spent in prayer each day. It is a different discipline altogether. For most people, talking to God throughout the day is not as satisfying as spending dedicated time in prayer. Once again, it is not one or the other. Both are good and need to be pursued.

Think of three married couples. The first spends all day texting each other, but they do not eat dinner together and do not see each other in the evening. The second couple does not text, but they eat dinner together in the evenings. The third couple texts throughout the day *and* eats dinner together. It is easy to guess which couple has the most satisfying relationship, but it is also easy to imagine that the couple that only has dinner together likely enjoys a deeper connection than the couple that only texts each other.

There are exceptions, of course. Some individuals do not have the capacity to manage a conversation over dinner with a loved one, and I doubt they are able to set aside time to have a conversation with God either. There are others whose season of life does not offer an opportunity to be alone in prayer on a regular basis because of life circumstances—like parenting small children, for example.

God's Grace for My Prayer Time

The next question I get is, "How much time should I set aside?" My response is simple: "Ask God; don't ask me!" It's my experience that God invites us into different rhythms in different seasons of our lives. It is not wrong or bad or a failure on our part if some people appear to be further than us in their prayer and spiritual lives. This is important to recognize because as we talk about various invitations to prayer, there is always a temptation to want what we think is best, often at the expense of what God is actually wanting for us at a given stage. James Martin, in his book *The Jesuit Guide to (Almost) Everything,* says that "all of us are newcomers to prayer, because our relationship with God changes over time and is constantly being renewed."[68] This means that we again and again find ourselves in the position of a beginner. One minister I know who mentors people in their prayer lives tells me he reminds everyone that the key is both consistency and variety. We need to look to God for grace to be consistent, and we need to not get stuck in ways of praying that stopped working a long time ago.

When my kids were young, I read a book about prayer that deeply inspired me. I decided to pray two hours a day. God had other ideas. One night I had a dream in which I was putting up a large tent in my backyard with a pastor friend of mine. It was so big, it went out beyond my yard and all the way across the street into my neighbor's yard. Then in the dream, I realized it was not my tent. It belonged to my friend who pastored a church in the area. To me, the symbolism was clear. It seemed God was saying I was not called to that much prayer; there was not enough space for it in the life he'd given me at the time. Others may be called to pray that much, especially someone in full-time ministry like my friend, but I was not.

Some ten years later, I had a very different dream. In it, I was trying to play a violin, but it was too small. Every time I began playing a tune, the violin slipped from my hands, interrupting the melody. A white-haired maestro came by and took the violin from me. He held it up, inspected it, and said, "This violin is too small for you. You have outgrown it. You need to ask your father for a bigger one."

The meaning of this dream was also unmistakable to me. My earthly father had wanted me to learn how to play the violin. That suggested to me that the dream was about something my heavenly father wanted badly for me. In the dream, the thing my earthly father wanted for me kept getting interrupted because it was not the right size. That in turn told me the dream was about something my heavenly father wanted for me, something that kept getting interrupted because it was not big enough. I immediately recognized its meaning: *my prayer time was not long enough.* I could see the correlation to my prayer time right away because by the time I would start to feel a connection with God in prayer, my prayer time would be over. This was the same as the pattern in the dream. I was just not setting aside enough time.

One quick note about dreams here. It is important to subject all dreams, visions, inner impressions, or any way we think God is speaking to us to the criteria for discernment described in the previous chapter.

For some reason, probably prompted by the Holy Spirit, I asked God how much time he wanted me to spend in prayer, rather than setting my own goals. Getting an answer from God on this was less difficult than I expected. I felt an inner conviction that God wanted at least forty-five minutes, but an hour would be better. It was clear to me also that this was in addition to spiritual reading time. This may sound radical to some, but once again, I strongly suggest that we go to God for his direction, not what we think or hear from others. He knows best his plans for each of us at different seasons of our lives.

What was even more valuable to me than simply knowing I needed to pray more were the words the maestro spoke: "You need to ask your father for a bigger violin." It seemed God was saying I needed to ask *him* for the grace to set aside that much time. It was not going to be something I could do on my own, which had been a problem in my previous attempts to extend my prayer time. I had tried to do it through sheer willpower and determination, and my efforts had failed miserably. What I needed was grace from God to pray, and God was inviting me to ask for it.

So, my second recommendation is that after we ask God to tell us how he is inviting us to pray, we then ask him for grace to respond. How do we ask God for grace to do this? I began to ask for the grace to pray five or ten minutes longer each week, until I reached what I felt was God's goal for me. If you sense God asking you to extend your prayer time, I suggest adding five or ten minutes at a time, incrementally each week.

Here are the steps I usually suggest that people follow:

1. First, know what you are aiming for by asking God what he wants for you.
2. Second, pray for the grace to do five minutes more than you are currently doing.
3. Try adding that extra five minutes of prayer time.
4. The following week, ask for the next five minutes and go back to Step 3. Repeat until you reach what God is inviting you into in Step 1 above.

The result for me in implementing this model was a tremendous blessing. My spiritual director had told me this would help me develop an affection for God, and he was right. I began to know what it was like to be a friend of God. What's more critical is that it helped me to establish that attachment to God we will discuss in greater detail in the next chapter.

Fifteen-Minute Frustration

It's helpful to anticipate the transitions in our growing prayer life. One of the first is what I call the fifteen-minute frustration. The fifteen-minute mark is probably the most precarious threshold I've personally experienced and also observed in the lives of many I have mentored over the years.

Many people, if not most, quit prayer when they reach the fifteen-minute mark. I think it's because praying less than that is not that difficult, so even if it's not satisfying or life-giving, we don't mind continuing the investment. What's more, if we pray less than fifteen minutes, God is usually inviting us to pray more, so we easily move from five to ten and then to fifteen. But if at the fifteen-minute mark it remains a chore rather than becoming life-giving, we begin to give up.

The reason fifteen minutes is not very satisfying in the long run is the same reason meeting a friend daily at a coffee shop for only fifteen minutes would not be very satisfying. It will work for a while, but then a pattern emerges in which by the time we settle down to talk about significant things, the time's up and we need to leave. Soon, we get frustrated and quit altogether.

Of course, there will be seasons in life when God invites us to pray for just fifteen minutes. And if those prayer times are structured and well-planned, fifteen minutes will be the right amount. But in many situations, having a deeper and more life-giving conversation on a regular basis will be difficult to do in fifteen minutes.

What If Prayer Time Is Dry?

The next obstacle that often stalls people's prayer growth is that their times with God feel dry, and they don't know why. Some focus on praying through lists and find that incredibly boring, in which case I strongly suggest not using a prayer list. Do not give in to feelings of "I should pray for" one thing or another. Focus instead on *what I want to talk to God about*. Talk with God about what you are feeling most intensely at that moment. Talk with him about your concerns, joys, successes, failures, and anything you feel strongly about that day.

As for the lists, I am not saying they are bad. For some highly structured personalities, they can be life-giving. Even for us who are less structured, praying through lists can have value, but it may be more helpful to have another time to do that, perhaps while doing something else like walking the dog or riding a stationary bike for exercise. God may also invite us to pray lists regularly in our prayer time, possibly in a more liturgical fashion, with the prayers written out in advance. But if that feels dry and not life giving, it may not be God's invitation, let's try to protect our dedicated time with God so that it's as life-giving as possible.

Another reason prayer feels dry at times is God may be inviting us to do something different than we're used to. Maybe we've outgrown the old pattern we've been using. If so, it's important to look for other ways to pray. There are as many ways to pray as there are people. Jesuit priest and author James Martin says, "No form of prayer is any better than another, any more than one way of being with a friend is better than another. What's better is what's best for you."[69] While it's important to be consistent in our prayer life, be flexible and open-minded in trying different things when necessary.

This brings us to the question of expectations. We've all been taught to expect prayer to look a certain way. Furthermore, we're conditioned by our own experiences—both positive and negative—as to what will feel life-giving and what will not. This is also a reflection of an intuitive sense that God has put in us that as we spend time with God, we will experience something positive.[70] I've even raised your expectations with this book. But as good and right as those expectations may be, they can lead to problems if they keep us locked into what we expect prayer to be like and we refuse God's invitation to other prayer practices he may have in mind. We're all tempted to put God in a box, but we must resist it. So, explore your expectations of what prayer time is to look and feel like, and then talk to God or a spiritual director as you re-evaluate those expectations.

The Role of Feelings

Some Christian traditions harbor a suspicion of feelings. To a degree, that suspicion is well-founded. We don't want our relationship with God to be solely based on feelings. If we experience dryness in our prayer times for a day or two, we need to press through. However, if it lasts two to three weeks, it is important to address the problem, either by asking God for help, trying something new, or talking with someone we think can help.

No one would think much about a married couple having strained communication for a day or two, but if the relational distance lasts two or three weeks, we'd agree it shouldn't be ignored or swept under the rug.

To extend the metaphor of marriage, what do you think about someone who would say: "I have dinner with my wife/husband because it's good for me. It's like going to the gym: I don't always want to go, but I do it because it's good for me." I've never heard anyone say that, but I have heard people say, "Personal spiritual practices are like going to the gym: I don't always want to do them, but I do them because they're good for me." I hope the irony is self-evident. Spending time with God should be more like the relational joy of having dinner with your spouse or close friend, not a task like going to the gym. If you have a task-oriented view of your relationship with God, consider thinking of it in more relational terms.

Distractions

Many people don't know how to handle distractions during prayer. But surprisingly, I rarely hear about problems with distraction from people who pray half an hour or more. And this may be the reason: if I pray for only ten minutes and I get distracted for five of those minutes, I've lost half my time and feel defeated.

A friend of mine describes his long-distance courtship with his wife-to-be while they were in college, long before cellphones. Their respective schools were two thousand miles apart. Letters were usually several pages long and dreamily gratifying, but phone calls were the pits! Depositing a handful of quarters into a payphone (when each quarter was worth $2.00 in today's money for these nearly broke students) bought no more than a few minutes of frustration. Every minute had to count—no romantic pauses.

Similarly, for someone who prays for only ten minutes, every minute needs to count. But for the person who prays for thirty minutes, even if they are distracted for five minutes, it's no big deal. The pressure is a lot less.

Some other commonsense suggestions include things like turning off your phone, closing the door to the room you're in, finding a quiet place, and keeping a notepad to write down a "to do" list. Creating that list by itself can have an anxiety-reducing benefit, but it also keeps a nagging thought from being distracting because we are worried we might forget to do something.

A more significant suggestion in dealing with distraction is to journal. Writing a letter to God helps us organize our thoughts and name our feelings and keeps us focused. The only limitation is that it takes a lot longer. We may go deeper, but we might cover fewer topics with God. A therapeutic advantage to journaling is that it creates integration between the left and right sides of the brain.[71] The left side processes information in a linear fashion and combines that with the right hemisphere, which encodes forms of memory that include subjective impressions, feelings, and sensations of experience.[72]

For some people, though, writing is a difficult activity, so there is no need to force that recommendation on anyone. Nonetheless, it is definitely worth a try, because for some people it ends up being an extremely life-giving practice.

Life Changes

I was surprised during my doctoral research at how often life changes stalled out people's prayer experience. Life is full of changes. Perhaps we get married, we change jobs, we have a baby, we have another baby, our baby begins teething, and so on. Each of these changes creates extensive interruptions in our routine and forces us into a different routine. Very often, this different routine at first does not include prayer. We may be going along fine in our prayer life until a change hits, and for a time we stop praying altogether because we can't figure out our new routine. This is where many people give up; they fall off the horse and can't figure out how to get back on.

It's important to anticipate these changes and know we will need to recreate a space for prayer in our new routines.

This is even true for weekdays versus weekends. The weekdays have a routine that weekends do not. People often feel guilty for not having the same prayer times on the weekends as they do during the week, but I don't think that's something to worry about. Ask God to show you if a different practice on the weekend is better in your situation. Maybe he's not as concerned about you spending a dedicated individual prayer time on the weekend if you're having five life-giving times during the week. As we grow in prayer, naturally our desire will increase to the point of *wanting* to pray on the weekends as well. In the meantime, we can ask God to continue to bless our prayer lives until we love to pray so much that not doing so on weekends feels unthinkable. In fact, for some people I have mentored, it seems the weekend offers more opportunity for a leisurely time of prayer, so that they can journal and pray for longer periods.

Guilt and Shame

One of the things that gets in the way of prayer for many people is the amount of guilt and shame they feel over their failure to spend time with God. You may even be feeling that discomfort just by reading this chapter. These feelings are so common and so pervasive, many people don't realize they're feeling guilt or shame until someone points it out to them.

For some, this is related to a need to change expectations, as discussed earlier in this chapter. For others, it is related to a sense of failure to achieve, described in Chapter 5. Whatever the reason, we need to make sure we address the shame and guilt. This can be done using the suggestions already described in those sections, but first we need to become aware that this is happening. Fortunately, that is not too difficult. Whenever we're feeling we *should* spend more time with God rather than actually *desiring* to spend more time with him, it is a flag we need to pay attention to.

Whenever feelings that we *should* pray more last longer than a week or two, we need to stop and reassess: Do we need to change our expectations? Do we need to monitor whether our motivation is to succeed for reasons other than God's invitation? Do we need to ask God for more grace? Do we need to ask him what to try next? Or maybe we should talk with a mentor or a spiritual director?

Chapter 10

Trusting God

I GREW UP IN BEIRUT, and I was there for the first three years of the Lebanese civil war in the 1970's. In Beirut most people live in apartments with balconies. Our apartment had exceptionally large balconies, where we sat outside when the weather was nice. Many balconies looked out on the streets, but ours did not. We were instead surrounded by other buildings about forty feet away, so it was relatively safe when there was no fighting going on.

Visiting and socializing is a big part of life in the Middle East. It became even more so during the early years of the war as life came to a standstill and neighbors got to know each other a lot more and visited each other regularly. Our balcony was one of the few in the area that overlooked some greenery, so we were popular with visitors. We'd sit out on lawn chairs and my mother would serve fruit and coffee to whoever was visiting. One day we were sitting out on the balcony, and it was time for the visitors to leave. We all walked them to the door and barely closed it behind them when there was a loud series of bangs—not explosions but more like gun shots—coming from our balcony.

We stepped back from the door, and on the tile in the middle of the living room, something was spinning loudly and fast like a top, but way too fast to see what it was. Eventually my father put his foot on it and stopped the spinning. It was a large caliber machine gun bullet that had gone astray. It entered between the buildings and ricocheted off our balcony wall a couple of times before landing in the living room and spinning on the floor. It had taken out a couple of small pieces of plaster from the balcony on its way. If the visitors had delayed by sixty seconds, someone would likely have been badly hurt or killed.

Does It Matter That God Is in Control?

Even though I felt fortunate that we were all safe and knew such stories encouraged other people's faith in God's sovereignty, it didn't necessarily increase my confidence in God's protection. It seemed I was missing something important. For years I thought that if I could figure out some satisfactory theology of the sovereignty of God, it would help me relax more and learn how to trust him. But this was hard for me to do. This world clearly seemed to be one of cause and effect, but how God remains in control while we as broken sinners have free will is a difficult challenge. Even though answers can be arrived at intellectually, for me these cognitive understandings were just not sufficient when it came to reassurance that God would spare me some awful illness. Dr. Karl Lehman says he has experienced much the same thing, whereby intellectual answers are not very helpful in helping people dealing with the effects of trauma.

However, I must admit that one reason this event did not strengthen my faith at the time was that my view of God's sovereignty was a bit anemic. I had a hard time seeing how

God was really in control. It seemed he had created a world where people were free to hurt others, where disease, accidents, wars, and famines were all part of this fallen world.

I began to ask God and others many questions and to look for answers from Christian authors. Observing a world of cause and effect where God does not seem to reliably intervene made life appear, at some emotional levels at least, out of control. Another stumbling block for many is that they grow up with simplistic or false theologies about God's protection from all harm unless they sin. They hear messages growing up about how God is a friend who would fight for you, never leave you, keep you from all harm, always be there for you. Then they go through some tragedy or tragedies where all of that seems completely false.

Jerry Bridges, in his book *Trusting God*, says we have to believe not only in God's love for us, but also in his sovereignty, and putting the two together helps us to develop trust.[73] I have great respect for Jerry Bridges, and I cannot argue with his thoughts, but I found that very difficult to implement. I believed it cognitively, but its impact on me emotionally speaking was limited.

Henri Nouwen, on the other hand, says it is only as we experience the love of God in prayer that we learn to truly trust him. I have learned that this is indeed the case. And I hope to describe how it was ultimately experiencing God in extended periods of prayer and developing friendship with him that helped me experience more of his love for me. In his book *Making Sense of Suffering*, Peter Kreeft asks whether any of our suffering really matters if we have God right beside us.[74] I would argue that if it stays at a cognitive level, it is relatively meaningless to know that God is right beside us. It is only as we experience him in a relationally comforting way that it begins to matter. Knowing that God is sovereign in a cognitive sense is not the same as having the faith to believe it in the deeper parts of one's being. Bridges' book was helpful to me in establishing good theology, but it did not help me develop the faith I needed in order for it to matter.

I remember one time driving home from work and asking God directly, "God, are you really in control?" I don't know what was different this time in my questioning, but this particular time, as I drove past a car dealership on a dark and cold Chicagoland winter evening, I felt the answer clearly: I was asking the wrong question. I sensed God saying, "The question is not whether I'm in control, it's whether I'm in charge."

That was an interesting distinction I had not thought of. I did not fully understand it yet—until one day I was reading *A New Kind of Christian* by Brian McLaren.[75] He says our view of God is driven by our modern lenses. In the case of God being in control, to the modern view this means the kind of robotic control exercised in a factory, where every movement to the smallest gear is controlled by a central computer. That is not what the Bible means by God being in control. The Scriptures describe God being in control like a king being sovereign, where a king does not micromanage everything in his realm. Instead, God as King has authority and jurisdiction over his realm. This is especially true in the lives of those who follow him and have given their lives over to seeking his Kingdom.

As I read what McLaren wrote, I remembered what God said on my drive sometime prior about him being *in charge*. Interestingly, a king in the mind of those who wrote Scripture would indeed be in charge, rather than in control, of every decision and transaction his subjects made.

What the king decreed happened, even though he did not decree every last thing in minute detail. In addition, he could be appealed to when something was not right for one of his citizens, or when his edicts were not adequately implemented. This is an important building block for our discussion of prayer because God can definitely be appealed to for any of our concerns, but first we have to be convinced that this is experientially true.

Experiencing God Consistently Answering Prayer

This building block of God answering prayer is not comforting to anyone who has not yet experienced it, or who has experienced it so intermittently that it does not make much difference. This is probably all of us at some point.

During my college years, I belonged to a student Christian fellowship that was very influential in my spiritual journey. They helped me come back to an adult version of my childhood faith. I had been a skeptical teenager when it came to faith, so I had stopped praying, but they told many stories of answered prayer, so I was inspired to try again. I prayed about many things, and not one of them was answered. I had heard all these great stories about how God answered prayers from students in that university Christian student group, so I tried, but I failed miserably. It got to a point where I seriously doubted that God answered any prayer at all. Once I looked up at the ceiling and said, "Hello, is there anyone there? Am I talking to the ceiling?" I'm sure I'm not the only one who found that my experience was not the same as what was claimed and taught around me. For many Christians, what they have been taught about prayer feels like platitudes that have nothing to do with their real-life experience.

I remember telling my university student ministry staff member at the time that I didn't think prayer worked because I had tried it for two years with zero results. I still remember his response: "If you come into a room and turn on a light switch and the light does not turn on, you don't think that electricity doesn't work; you rather ask what is wrong that it's not working." Of course, that presupposes that we've experienced electric lighting as reliable before, which did not translate to my experience with prayer, since I had not experienced it as working at all, let alone reliably. The analogy is nonetheless helpful, because we can rely on what the Scriptures say, and we can see it in the lives of other Christians around us who witness to its reality. This helps us to continue to experiment, to ask others, and to read what others have experienced. In doing so, we begin the journey of transforming seeming platitudes into real understanding with personal nuances grown out of our own experiences, acknowledging questions we still have, and through it all growing in faith that prayer is transforming us and our relationship with God.

As people grow in prayer, I have found they experience a greater increase in God's answers to prayer. Perhaps it's because there is a greater maturity in what they ask for, which aligns more clearly with God's will and desires in their lives. Perhaps it's because they grow in righteousness as well, and the dynamic applies that James refers to in James 5:16: "The prayer of a righteous person is powerful and effective."

Of course, this does not mean that being more invested in prayer or being more righteous saves anyone from the sufferings in this world. At worst, sometimes people are simply taught bad theology. One example is the "health and wealth" gospel, where Jesus' invitation to follow him is turned into a selfish formula for health and wealth. The implication (and sometimes even the spoken condemnation) is that if you're not healthy and wealthy, it's probably because you don't have enough faith or are doing something wrong. This can lead to beliefs that if we pray hard enough, we can hold suffering at bay. This was partly my story that I relayed in Chapter 2, where I thought that if I prayed for God to protect my kids from a list of things, they would be safe, and I would no longer feel anxious. But as I described, this approach can create even more anxiety and can interfere in our relationship with God.

Rather, prayer should create a greater confidence that we are in God's care, that he will either change the circumstance or give us what we need to change it or endure it. My spiritual director at one time—retired pastor Dennis Anderson—has been practicing Centering Prayer for twenty years, twice a day for twenty-five minutes each. He tells me that it has created in him a reservoir of peace that has increased his confidence in God, allowing him to be able to trust that no matter what happens, he will have what is needed when it is needed.

A child attaches to a parent through thousands of complex interactions and develops a pattern of attachment as a result. Sometimes it is a healthy pattern—if the parent is consistently attuned to the child and the child develops what is called a *secure* attachment. Otherwise, the child can feel anxious and develop an *insecure, avoidant,* or *disorganized* attachment. These patterns get activated unconsciously later in life in all our relationships.[76] These patterns of attachment affect the parts of the brain that control anxiety and how it is soothed.[77] How we experienced attachment as children has an impact on our level of anxiety. In addition, parents also pass on to their children phobias and anxieties that they may not even be aware of. In the case of my own mother, she inherited the anxieties of her mother around health and loss because of the trauma my grandmother experienced in losing so many children. I in turn inherited my mother's fears of illness without even realizing it. I did not even know I had any fear of illness until I had my own children and began worrying ceaselessly about their health.

The good news is that we can experience healing from all of this. The attachment patterns we developed as children can change in counseling. But they can also change through personal prayer, which can create a space to experience a new healing attachment to God.

Thousands of interactions related to physical and emotional needs mold a child's attachment with their parent or caregiver, hopefully characterized by dependability and love. Similarly, as we increase our relationship and connection with God, we attach to God as dependable and loving.

Attachment and What Happens When God Doesn't Answer

One of the building blocks of the theory of attachment is the concept of a "secure base." It was developed by Dr. Mary Salter Ainsworth in her study of mother-infant interactions in Uganda in the 1950's and then later in white middle-class homes of Baltimore, Maryland. She observed that a child feels a sense of security around the parent they are attached to, and from that sense of security, they can take risks to explore the world around them and return to the secure base for comfort and stability.[78]

Dr. John Bowlby, one of the pioneers of the psychological theory of attachment, gives us a view of how healthy parents provide a secure base for their children as they grow. He describes . . .

> . . . the provision by both parents of a secure base from which a child or an adolescent can make sorties into the outside world and to which he can return knowing for sure that he will be welcomed when he gets there, nourished physically and emotionally, comforted if distressed, reassured if frightened.[79]

Similarly, the development of a secure base by deepening our attachment to God can happen in many ways. God is not limited to one or two ways of doing this. I have noticed, for example, that Catholics who go to daily Mass seem to experience a secure base; others who do Immanuel Prayer with someone on a regular basis report experiencing it as well.

In the previous chapter on hindrances to prayer, I described a shift in my own prayer life where God was telling me I had outgrown the time I used to spend in prayer, and he was inviting me to ask for grace to pray longer. When I responded to that invitation, the length of time I spent with God began to exceed thirty to forty-five minutes. This expanded time allowed me to share more deeply with God all that I was feeling and what I needed in a deeper way. This experience of God as one who is there allowed me to experience his closeness and comfort on a regular basis. This made me want to spend even more time with him. In addition, I began to experience his answers to prayer more consistently than I had ever before. This brought about a new sense of safety. I do not claim that it healed me completely by any means, but I believe it reduced the overall anxiety baseline in my life. It created at some level a little bit more serenity and equanimity and, most importantly, it deepened my relationship with God. It created a sense of trust I had tried to cultivate intellectually for years with limited success.

Some of the research on prayer bears out this connection between increased investment in prayer and deeper and longer-lasting changes to the brain. Newberg and Waldman write, "Neurologically, we have found that the longer one prays or meditates, the more changes occur in the brain. Five minutes of prayer once a week may have little effect, but forty minutes of daily practice, over a period of years, will bring permanent changes to the brain."[80]

This deepening of the relationship is critical when God does not answer prayer. When bad things happen, as we saw in the chapter on trauma, we need the presence of a caring person to give us attunement so that we can get through it without being overwhelmed, with some underlying sense of God's love and care, and grow from it rather than be damaged by it. If we are convinced experientially that God will be there, helping us to get through things without being traumatized, then we have a drop in the overall level of anxiety.

If we can draw some conclusions, then, about attaching to God through increased prayer, it might look like this: As we grow and deepen in our prayer life, we experience more of God's nearness and comfort, which then increases our desire to spend more time with him. We also begin to see more and more of his activity. This increases our faith in his involvement in our lives and willingness to act on our behalf. This does not necessarily heal anxiety, but it reduces some of the sense of a chaotic, out-of-control universe and allows us to grow in trusting God. What's more is that even from a purely psychological point of view, this kind of attachment is ideal. In the words of John Bowlby, the attachment pioneer:

> Throughout adult life the availability of a responsive attachment figure remains the source of a person's feeling secure. All of us, from the cradle to the grave, are happiest when life is organized as a series of excursions, long or short, from the secure base provided by our attachment figure(s).[81]

Isn't that what God's heart is for us? To experience this with him? Until I started experiencing this kind of attachment with God, I never understood 1 John 4:18: "There is no fear in love. But perfect love drives out fear, because fear has to do with punishment. The one who fears is not made perfect in love."

Problems Areas

I wish I could say it is always this simple. Unfortunately, as mentioned earlier, there are many ways in which children may have their attachment and sense of secure base damaged. This not only makes them more susceptible to anxiety later in life but also shapes their relationship with God.[82]

The good news is that a secure attachment can be developed later in life,[83] often in therapy. Trauma can create blocks in our relationship with God and our ability to trust him. Dealing with those blocks becomes important so our ability to trust God can grow unimpeded.

In Chapter 6 we talked about two important aspects of the pain processing pathway proposed by Drs. Lehman and Wilder. One was the need to receive attunement, which we discussed in that chapter, and the other was to correctly interpret the negative events, which we will now address.

Often in trauma, the thing that causes anxiety to linger is not so much the traumatic event itself, but how it changes our interpretation of reality. You may recall in Chapter 6 we talked about how Jane continued to misinterpret her husband's phone use. In some ways, therapy can provide the safe space to rebuild the narrative of what happened. This helps identify false beliefs that were held before the trauma or that crept in during the traumatic event or afterward, as well as bring closure to the traumatic event itself.

Here's another example. This one is theoretical but all too common, with individual variations. Suppose someone is walking down a street that seems safe and sees two guys walking toward him who appear normal and unthreatening . . . until they attack and rob him. The resulting anxiety in this person is not so much a direct fear of being mugged, but rather a shaken confidence in his understanding of the world he thought was relatively safe.

These traumas and the false beliefs they engender can become obstacles to trusting God with the parts of our lives affected by the given trauma. Therapy and inner healing prayer with others are tools God gives us to deal with those obstacles. In conjunction with those tools, we can also find some measure of healing in our personal prayer through deepening secure attachment that will also deepen our relationship with God in the process, changing our view of the world from a place of low attunement and high insecurity that the traumatized can experience, into a place of attunement and secure attachment.

Chapter 11

Anxiety Changes Our Brain; Prayer Also Changes It

IN THE FIELD OF NEUROSCIENCE, knowledge of how anxiety disorders are reflected in the brain has been growing rapidly in recent years, thanks in large parts to advances in the technology of brain imagery. Even though what is available is complex, continuously developing, and beyond the scope of this book, one or two examples can help us develop some useful insights. Some of what I want to share gets rather technical, so put on your seatbelt and hang in there. Or, if it doesn't interest you, bail out and skip to the next section of this chapter.

Changes in the Brain

We do know that the brains of individuals who show reasonable levels of integration between the different parts of the brain experience less anxiety.[84] We also know that genetics, trauma, and parent-child interactions, as well as attachment,[85] can contribute to changes in the brain that make it more anxious.[86] One example is that in brains that are more anxious, elements of what is called the *limbic system*, or the emotional brain, can be larger than those same elements in non-anxious brains. Anxious individuals may also have a deficiency of *serotonin*, a chemical that is involved in transmitting signals between brain cells. This causes the brain to focus on negative information and therefore produce more anxiety.[87]

Sometimes the cognitive thinking part of our brain ruminates on anxiety-provoking thoughts and beliefs. When the amygdala's connection to that part of the brain senses this, it begins to ring the alarms of anxiety. More commonly, anxiety starts with an outside event. Our brains get sensory information from the eyes, nose, mouth, skin, and ears through a brain structure called the *thalamus*. From there, it travels along a very fast connection to the *amygdala*.[88] The amygdala is a small structure in the limbic system that is particularly implicated in anxiety disorders. It is the alarm system of the brain. At the same time, the thalamus sends a concurrent signal to the thinking brain. However, this second signal and how it is processed and responded to is much slower (about half a second) than that going through the amygdala.[89] It's a little bit like stepping out into the street at dusk in an unfamiliar area and realizing you are in front of a truck coming your way that you hadn't noticed. You want your brain to immediately tell you to jump and get out of the way, rather than spend time analyzing the information, by which time you might be dead.

When the amygdala receives the signal from the thalamus, it quickly evaluates it to see if it should sound the alarm for you to jump. But even though it functions as an alarm system, the amygdala can also be calmed down. The simultaneous but slower signal being processed by your thinking brain may reveal that the truck you thought was coming at you is in fact stationary, or maybe nothing more than a life-size picture of a truck on billboard. The thinking brain then sends the signal to the amygdala to calm down. Once it is told to calm down in a particular context, the amygdala can also learn not to sound the alarm the next time a similar situation arises.[90]

The calming of the amygdala is done by signals from the *prefrontal cortex*. That is an area of our brain that does our adult reasoning, among other things. More specifically, the calming is mediated by a structure near the prefrontal cortex called the *anterior cingulate cortex*, which we mentioned earlier is involved in gratitude and regulating emotions. As the amygdala is calmed, the next time it evaluates a similar alarm, it will no longer need to be reassured; it will have learned there is nothing to worry about. This is in theory what happens with exposure therapy: the amygdala learns that the stimulus that rang the alarm is not dangerous, and therefore does not ring the alarm the next time it gets that signal. Or if the alarm goes off, it is quickly and more effectively calmed.

In an imaging study done after psychotherapy for PTSD, it was shown that the anterior cingulate cortex had higher levels of activation than before the treatment.[91] In other words, the therapy helped it function better.

Imaging studies have also shown that children who suffer from PTSD have an enlarged amygdala, and their prefrontal cortex is diminished in size.[92] Similarly, imaging of the brains of Vietnam veterans suffering from PTSD showed decrease of blood flow in the prefrontal cortex compared to those not suffering from PTSD when exposed to traumatic pictures and sounds.[93] This could mean that part of what makes a brain anxious relates to enlarged and hypersensitive structures and changed chemistry, as well as a failure in the ability to bring calm from the thinking brain after an anxious thought sets in.[94]

The Good News about Prayer

Just as anxiety and other influences change our brain in negative ways, therapy and medication can bring positive changes.[95] So can prayer. In its various forms, prayer can mold and shape our brain in positive ways over weeks, months, and even years. For instance, in their book *How God Changes Your Brain*, neuroscientist Andrew Newberg and therapist Mark Robert Waldman note that spiritual practices seem to strengthen the *anterior cingulate*, which, as described in Chapter 1, helps to regulate emotion.[96] In addition, a well-developed and connected prefrontal cortex will do a better job in calming down the amygdala, and we can develop that through contemplative practices that will be described in this chapter and the next.[97]

Mindfulness

Jon Kabat-Zinn made Buddhist meditation available to a broad audience through his program called "Mindfulness Based Stress Reduction." As you may remember from Chapter 1, Kabat-Zinn defines mindfulness as "the awareness that emerges through paying attention on purpose, in the present moment, and nonjudgmentally to the unfolding experience."[98] This principle is foundational to any type of meditation, and Kabat-Zinn was not the first or the last person to study its health benefits. Mental health therapies have followed in his footsteps, such as Mindfulness Based Cognitive Therapy, Dialectic Behavior Therapy, and Acceptance and Commitment Therapy. Each of these therapies changes our brain in beneficial ways (though our understanding of how different therapies change the brain is only beginning[99]). For best results, they generally require daily time invested in the practices they teach.

Christian traditions have various meditative and contemplative practices. Sometimes the terms' definitions are reversed from those of Eastern religions. In some Western Christian spiritual traditions, the meaning of *contemplation* is equivalent to *meditation* in Eastern religious traditions. Sometimes the definitions are not consistent within Christian contexts. But the bigger issues are not terminology but theology—specifically, whether or not God is the focus. Similar practices may come out of Christianity and Eastern religions, but they have different ideological and theological frameworks. But do they have a similar or different effect on the brain? Could they provide similar therapeutic benefits? Or is one more beneficial than the other?

As it turns out, at least according to one study where secular mindfulness practices were compared with religious ones, people engaged in contemplative practices within the framework of their religious beliefs experienced less anxiety and depression.[100] Remember the role of the prefrontal cortex in calming anxiety? A study of Franciscan nuns who had been practicing Centering Prayer for fifteen years showed that there was increased blood flow to the prefrontal cortex during their prayer times.[101] In addition, at least according to Newberg and Waldman, the more you believe in what you are meditating or praying about, the greater impact it will have.[102]

The case for Christian prayer

I can already see the gears turning as you read this: Is this book really saying that all Christian prayer does is change your brain? Absolutely not! God is at work with us in prayer. Eugene Peterson, who gave us *The Message* paraphrase of the Bible, says that prayer happens in the "middle voice": neither is it completely our action, nor are we completely passive to God's action. Rather we "become subjects in an action in which we are personally involved." We have our part to play, and so does God; we are actors together forming the outcome. We do not change ourselves, but we engage with God to be changed.[103]

The benefit of secular meditative practices that change our brain are limited compared to Christian ones. Secular mindfulness exercises have no eternal value in and of themselves, whereas prayer has eternal value. Christian prayer benefits our relationship with Jesus, not to mention the eternal rewards for prayer he promised us in Matthew 6:6: "But when you pray, go into your room, close the door and pray to your Father, who is unseen. Then your Father, who sees what is done in secret, will reward you."

In summary, then, while anxiety may change our brain in negative ways, God wants to transform it for the better. We can cooperate with him in this by responding to his invitations to pray in the ways he thinks are most appropriate for each season of life.

Mindfulness Comparisons

Given the empirically established benefits of secular practices of mindfulness, I believe it's helpful to leverage these findings as we evaluate which prayer practices from various Christian traditions can be most helpful in reducing anxiety.

Attention to thoughts

The first thing we note in mindfulness-based therapies is the focus on exercising some control over our thoughts. We know Scripture encourages us to do this as well. In Philippians 4:8, Paul exhorts us as follows: "Finally, brothers and sisters, whatever is true, whatever is noble, whatever is right, whatever is pure, whatever is lovely, whatever is admirable—if anything is excellent or praiseworthy—think about such things."

For someone with an overactive brain, the anxiety and speed of their thoughts is so intense, the idea of trying to exercise control over them and their strong emotions may seem not only foreign but completely out of the realm of possibility. Yet whether we have an overactive brain or not, the practice of meditative or contemplative prayers has specific benefits regarding control of thoughts. Newberg and Waldman's review of the scientific findings shows that advanced meditators have the ability to control other parts of their brains. I have personally found this to be true. As I practiced Centering Prayer, I found it easier at other times when I was distracted to refocus my attention on what I needed to pay attention to.[104] As we will discuss in the next chapter, these types of prayers can help to move us in the positive direction of exercising some control over our racing thoughts. Not only that, but as Curt Thompson says, "All of the spiritual disciplines both require and support the skill of mindful attention, which enables us to set our minds on the Spirit."[105]

Neutrality and radical acceptance

Secular mindfulness may encourage us to see everything with a neutral lens, without labeling things as good or bad. For those who are deeply wounded and who get triggered easily, this can have some benefit. If everything is regarded as neutral, there's less to be anxious about. The next step in secular mindfulness is known as "radical acceptance," an uncompromising acceptance of reality.

We discussed the role of acceptance in our relationship with God and its psychological benefits in Chapter 2. When it comes to neutrality, Buddhism teaches that life has pain, which is unavoidable, but it is our response to pain that creates suffering. But consider once again what we learn from the responses of Jesus and Paul, who, by the example they set, tell us that when we experience something negative, we don't have to redefine the pain as something neutral. Rather we can take a mental step beyond the pain and believe God can transform the event to render redemptive value through it. The Christian perspective calls us to accept the cross that God gives us, to patiently endure the trials that we experience—not with neutrality, but with the powerful hope of redemption and ultimately resurrection.

Good and bad detachment

The third aspect of mindfulness we want to look at is the principle of detachment. While mindfulness recognizes both our thoughts and feelings, it maintains we are not simply the sum of our thoughts and feelings. Keeping this in mind helps when we become overly anxious. It's easy to label ourselves as "anxious" people, but that's not very useful. Recognizing and reminding ourselves that we are *not* our thoughts and feelings, but rather we *have* these thoughts and feelings, helps to create some detachment.

Some Buddhist practitioners attempt to avoid attachment to anything or anyone, although some would argue that's not what true Buddhist detachment is about.

In Buddhism, just as in Christianity, popular belief and practice sometimes deviates from established orthodoxy. We had a Korean friend, for example, who told us that her Buddhist grandmother believed she should try not to get overly attached to people.

From a Christian perspective, there is definitely a call to detachment, but it's a different kind of detachment. Jesus calls us to detach ourselves from anything that keeps us from him. For instance, Ignatius of Loyola, the founder of the Jesuits, encouraged his followers to pray for the grace of detachment from anything other than God's will. He called this "holy indifference." As a result of that practice, Ignatius developed a sense of peace and serenity. Later in life, he said that if the pope ordered the dissolution of the ministry he'd spent his life building, it would take him about fifteen minutes to compose himself.[106]

It makes me wonder, if we had God's grace for that kind of detachment, what would that do to our anxiety levels? I remember one period in my life when career advancement meant more to me than it should have. At the same time, it was a period of significant growth in prayer. I found myself having said something awkwardly in a meeting that I perceived to hurt my chances of a promotion. I remember walking out of that meeting feeling anxious and very annoyed with myself. Yet I was quickly able to remind myself that I wanted this promotion only if God wanted it for me. Embracing that perspective was growth in detachment and holy indifference. I then told myself that if God wanted it, then a badly worded sentence in a high visibility meeting was not too hard for God to correct. I found myself surprised that the anxiety subsided. It seems my investment in prayer had improved my prefrontal cortex's ability to calm my amygdala in this situation.

Three Types of Meditation

One significant practice that is encouraged in almost all mindfulness-based therapies is meditation. Christians have various reactions to that term and to the practice. But since this is not a book about non-Christian meditation, I do want to examine some types of Christian meditation that I believe can be helpful in developing spiritual health when dealing with anxiety. One of my seminary professors, Dr. James Wilhoit, would say regularly that the Bible describes three models of meditation. The first is meditating on Scripture, the second is meditating on creation, and the third is meditating on God's providence.

Meditating on Scripture

Before we dive into meditation, I want to say that any kind of regular engagement with Scripture, whether it be reading it, studying it, memorizing it, or meditating on it using any of the techniques below, will likely accomplish benefits in cognitive restructuring. It will help to train our brain not to think in ways that contribute to anxiety unnecessarily. It will build our faith and continue to nourish us spiritually when we need it most.

Historically, there have been many ways to meditate on Scripture and variations on each of those. But here, in the simplest forms, are three models I find most helpful.

Lectio Divina is almost as old as the church. It involves multiple readings of the same text (usually a short passage), each with a different emphasis—silence, reading, meditation, prayerful response, and finally contemplation and rest. **Silence:** Take time to quiet your mind and rest in God's presence for a short period. **Read:** Read the text slowly and out loud, and see where the Holy Spirit draws your attention (linger on any words and see what the Holy Spirit is saying to you). **Meditate:** Read the text again out loud, focusing on where you feel God inviting you. Let the invitation sink in, trying not to slip into analysis mode. **Respond:** Read the text a third time. Now respond to God in prayer about what he has invited you into, talking to him about what feelings come up for you. **Rest:** Take some time to simply rest in God and allow him to deepen those themes in your spirit.[107]

Luther's Garland. Martin Luther's barber once asked him how to pray, and Luther wrote down this method in response. It involves reading with an eye to learning, giving thanks, repenting, and petitioning.[108] **Instruction:** What is the text teaching us? **Thanksgiving:** How does what I learned cause me to praise and give thanks to God? **Confession:** How does this cause me to repent? How does this bring up feelings of lament over my brokenness and sin? How does it encourage me to get back on a more life-giving path? **Petition:** What does the text suggest I pray? In what way is the Holy Spirit guiding me to pray?

Scripture Imagination is an exercise taught by the Jesuits and others. It involves letting the Holy Spirit use the power of our imagination to bring the text alive in fresh ways. **Read** a text of Scripture. **Imagine** you are part of the scene, part of the story. What are you seeing? What are the colors, shapes, sizes, motions? What do you hear? What are you smelling? What can you sense? The wind? The silence? The roughness of the path you are walking on? **Look** at your thoughts and feelings. Where do you see harmony or dissonance? **Press** into that harmony or dissonance with God. What is the Word saying to you in that experience?[109]

Meditating on creation

Spending time in nature causes our prefrontal cortex to integrate better with the rest of our brain.[110] As we saw in Chapter 1, this is helpful in dealing with anxiety because the connections from the prefrontal cortex to the amygdala are the pathways that calm our anxiety levels. Here are three ways to meditate on creation I've found most helpful.

First, simply take a walk in a nature setting. In my younger years, I complained to my spiritual director that I was going through a blank period in prayer. Prayer just didn't emerge from my heart or mind; I had too many things on my mind. He suggested I take a walk in a garden. I took his advice and, I must admit, thirty years later, his suggestion has not yet failed me once. Being outside always seems to break whatever stuck place I find myself in. I begin to pray as I walk, and the prayers flow naturally.

A second way is to enter into silence to engage with God. Have a seat in a garden, or somewhere with a view of nature. You don't have to pray or speak anything. Allow yourself mental rest. When thoughts come to mind, observe them. When you leave the silence, journal about the experience.

Third, try listening to God through nature itself. This can be done by walking or sitting still in nature. During one such walk, I was feeling inadequate for a greater role in ministry I felt God was calling me to. Previous painful episodes in ministry seemed to keep me from stepping into all that God was inviting me into. As I walked, I came upon a fallen tree that had been struck by lightning. Except it only fell a few feet and then was caught in the Y-shaped branch of another tree, which supported it and kept it upright. I sensed internally this tree image was significant for me. God was encouraging me with a symbolism from nature. Even though I may experience brokenness, he will provide the support necessary to accomplish all he asks of me.

Meditating on God's providence

Gratitude for God's redemption when things are going well and also in the middle of hard times is another form of meditation. We established in Chapter 2 how gratitude can work in the Anxiety Redemption Prayer, and how it creates in our bodies the right conditions for a deeper connection with God. Paul, of course, encourages us to "give thanks in all circumstances" (1 Thess. 5:18), and most models of prayer incorporate thanksgiving at some level. My encouragement here would be to expand the time dedicated to thanksgiving. Try thanking God for different things each day as this can increase your awareness of all the things God has given you and provided for you.

Beyond meditating the way Scripture tells us, there is also the question of contemplation. As mentioned previously the terms *contemplation* and *meditation* may mean different things depending on the religious tradition. For our purposes, in the next chapter we will explore forms of contemplative Christian prayer, which are more analogous to mindfulness meditation. Semantics aside, the move from conversational prayers to prayers that go deeper than words is a strong part of Christian traditions.

Chapter 12

Three Prayers for Meditation

SOMETIME AROUND 2006, I FELT GOD CALLING ME to a more contemplative prayer practice. My conversational prayer life had been so life giving, I hesitated, fearing I might have to give up some of the benefits of conversational prayer. It wasn't an either/or choice, but interestingly, I found it harder and harder to pray conversationally. When I sat down to pray and tried to speak, I felt a strong need to be silent. It was like being in a symphony orchestra hall, with a brief pause in the music, where words or sounds of any kind were just not appropriate.

Was I just tongue-tied, or was this an invitation from the Holy Spirit to explore meditation more deeply? At first it was uncomfortable because I had so many questions about whether classic meditation was really "Christian."

But I discovered that the emphasis on meditation in secular mindfulness should not leave followers of Jesus on the defensive, trying to find a Christian equivalent. There is a surprisingly universal thread through almost all monastic Christian traditions where an experience of joyful—euphoric even—union with God takes place during meditation. Sometimes this happens after long periods of contemplation, and at other times happens after relatively short periods. This ultimate unitive experience is desirable, but it is not the goal. Rather, the goal is simply faithfulness to God's invitation to be with him in a space beyond words, in near complete internal silence. Spiritual directors know that this invitation seems to come to those on a prayer journey at different times, and they can help discern it with them. Our faithfulness in responding to this invitation can have a beneficial effect on our overall levels of anxiety.

In addition to the three types of meditation on Scripture explained in the previous chapter, Christian tradition offers us three traditional prayers ideal for contemplation: the Jesus Prayer, the Breath Prayer, and Centering Prayer. The latter two should probably not be attempted by those for whom focusing on breathing might be triggering, such as those with asthma or other similar conditions.

The Jesus Prayer

The Jesus Prayer comes from the Orthodox church. It is found in Luke 18:9-14, the Parable of the Pharisee and the Tax Collector.

> To some who were confident of their own righteousness and looked down on everyone else, Jesus told this parable:
> "Two men went up to the temple to pray, one a Pharisee and the other a tax collector. The Pharisee stood by himself and prayed: 'God, I thank you that I am not like other people—robbers, evildoers, adulterers—or even like this tax collector. I fast twice a week and give a tenth of all I get.'

"But the tax collector stood at a distance. He would not even look up to heaven, but beat his breast and said, *'God, have mercy on me, a sinner* [emphasis added].'

"I tell you that this man, rather than the other, went home justified before God. For all those who exalt themselves will be humbled, and those who humble themselves will be exalted."

I know some post-Reformation Protestants may feel resistance to the idea of continuously asking God for mercy. It brings up images of sin and forgiveness, and Protestants are taught that sin has already been dealt with on the cross and full forgiveness is received at the point of believing in Jesus as Savior and choosing to follow him. Therefore, continually repenting feels inconsistent with that belief.

However, when I was in my twenties and thirties, I had a Jesuit spiritual director. I asked him a similar question. His response stayed with me. He said the word "mercy" in this prayer encompasses much more than forgiveness of sin. He helped me understand that God's mercy permeates everything, and so this prayer is meant to encompass God's mercy in all the different ways it is manifested.

Many years later I was reading Eugene Peterson's book *A Long Obedience in the Same Direction,* and he essentially said the same thing. God is always active in mercy, so when we pray this prayer, we are asking for more of God's activity in our lives:

"Mercy, GOD, mercy!": the prayer is not an attempt to get God to do what he is unwilling otherwise to do, but a reaching out to what we know that he does do, an expressed longing to receive what God is doing in and for us in Jesus Christ. . . .

The word *mercy* means that the upward look to God in the heavens does not expect God to stay in the heavens but to come down, to enter our condition, to accomplish the vast enterprise of redemption, to fashion in us his eternal salvation.[111]

The Breath Prayer

In secular mindfulness, breathing is emphasized. There is a basic physiological reason as breathing slowly and deeply reduces anxiety. Part of our nervous system that activates our fight or flight reflex is called the *sympathetic nervous system*. Its counterpart is the *parasympathetic nervous system*, does the opposite by shutting down the fight or flight reflex.

Think of the sympathetic nervous system as the gas pedal on your car and the parasympathetic as the brakes. When you push on the gas pedal, your body activates to deal with the threat you are perceiving. When the threat is gone, the body decides there is no more threat to deal with, you push the brake, and that activates your parasympathetic nervous system, which calms things down, effectively reducing anxiety.

The sympathetic and parasympathetic systems aren't usually active at the same time; one is always more dominant than the other. When we engage in slow deep breathing, we increase the activity of the vagus nerve, a part of the parasympathetic nervous system that controls the activity of many internal organs. This reduces anxiety. The only problem is that it's short acting, and we need to keep doing it over and over again. The slowing down that occurs from slow deep breathing is beneficial in reducing anxiety, so it's not surprising then that it's been used by different religious traditions to increase inner peace and awareness during prayer.

The Hesychast monastic tradition in the Eastern Orthodox church ties the Jesus Prayer described earlier to breathing. In this tradition, and in Orthodox monastic traditions in general, they use this prayer in obedience to Paul's injunction in 1 Thessalonians 5:17 to "pray continually."

The prayer can be shortened to one word, "Jesus," or "mercy," or "Lord," wherever you want the emphasis to be. Or the Jesus Prayer can be said in its full length: "Lord Jesus Christ, Son of God, have mercy on me, a sinner." Praying the first part of the prayer while inhaling and the other part exhaling works well. Or you can say the whole thing (mentally) with each breath in and then again with each breath out.

When I'm anxious about something, I find the Jesus Prayer works well for me, especially when I combine it with a prayer walk. After I walk about a mile or so, emphasizing the Lordship of Christ, feeling the supernatural power of his name, pressing into his mercy, I start to feel held and upheld by God. This creates a sense of reassurance in his sovereignty. No matter what transpires, God will use it for good. I may experience that goodness either directly because it appears obviously good, or with faith in his providence that God will redeem it for good even if the interim suffering is beyond my understanding.

Call to Centering Prayer

I had read much about Centering Prayer during my training in spiritual direction, but I had a lot of questions.

Let me describe it first, then share how God helped me deal with my initial objections.

To begin Centering Prayer, sit in a comfortable position with a straight back. Avoid having fingers intercrossed or legs crossed due to the distraction of legs or fingers going numb. The recommendation is to use a timer for twenty minutes twice a day or thirty minutes once a day.

Choose a sacred word, like "love" or "Jesus" or "peace." Close your eyes and repeat that word to focus your mind on God. Distracting thoughts will inevitably arise, but use your chosen sacred word to bring your thoughts gently back to God. The sacred word is not a mantra, we don't have to keep saying it and can stop as soon as we feel centered on God. It also helps to focus on breathing to stay centered. Some suggest imagining distracting thoughts as items on a river that flows by.

One problem I had for a long time is that by trying to focus on God, my mind went to attributes of God, or to images of him as creator or Isaiah's vision of the throne room, and so on. This became very distracting. I found it helpful to find that some people suggested focusing on my breathing instead and on God's presence in breath, given that the word for spirit and breath in the Old Testament are the same. I found that in doing this, I became aware at some point of God's presence in the silence. And whether I became aware or not, it did not matter; the main goal was to make space for him in silence.

I've found this practice to be fruitful in my life, but initially I had many questions and I was resistant. Hopefully, as I share these you might find answers to some of your own questions.

Is it just a mental exercise?

I needed to resolve whether this was just a mental exercise or a form of Eastern meditation or genuine Christian prayer. Initially, I felt like I was exercising my mind instead of my spirit, because I didn't really experience God at all. This lifted when I stopped trying to *make* myself experience God and instead simply surrendered my time, believing that God was somehow at work in me. Sometimes I sensed his presence, and other times I didn't, but my role was simply to show up, and the rest was God's responsibility. That was very freeing.

The biggest difference, I finally came to realize, between a mental exercise of concentration and Centering Prayer is the presence and activity of the Holy Spirit. If I calm my mind enough to be aware of the Holy Spirit inside me and nurture that awareness, that is a very different thing than merely teaching my mind to focus. One calms my brain, the other takes it a step further to open me to greater connection with the Holy Spirit in my inmost being.

But could it be Eastern meditation disguised as Christian?

The first difference my seminary professors helped me see was that Eastern meditation is about a complete emptying of the psyche, whereas in Centering Prayer there is no emptying of the self but instead a focus on God.

The second difference is that Eastern meditation describes a kind of union with the universe that is like a drop of water in the ocean, wherein one's identity is lost during meditation. In Centering Prayer, on the other hand, people can have highly joyful experiences of connecting with God and feeling a oneness with him, without ever feeling a loss of identity.

A third difference between the two is that Christian meditation is a response to God's invitation, whereas Eastern meditation is pursued proactively to perfect one's consciousness. In his book *When the Well Runs Dry*, Father Thomas Green, a Jesuit spiritual director, talks about the need to be careful in discerning this difference.[112] In Centering Prayer, we surrender to God working in us. Earlier Eugene Peterson explained in his book *The Contemplative Pastor* that prayer is more than us speaking and God listening, or God speaking and us listening. There is also our participation in God's action on us when we pray as described earlier.[113] That concept is true no matter what kind of prayer we are engaged in, but it is most acutely true with Centering Prayer.

What if God speaks?

I was also concerned not to ignore inner impressions that might be from God. In listening to God in prayer, we pay attention to inner impressions or mental pictures that we sense are from God rather than our own psyche. However, in Centering Prayer, most practitioners would agree we do not pay attention to those impressions or mental pictures; we let them go just like any other distractions.

At first this felt quasi-blasphemous to me. And some practitioners of Centering Prayer do stop and write down things they sense to be from God. Others, however, are strongly opposed to the idea.

This is one area where I am once again grateful for my seminary professor Dr. David Sherbino, who reassured me that if God wanted to let me know something, he would get my attention. I decided that Dr. Sherbino was right. God had a good track record of getting my attention when he needed to, so I would dedicate this time to simply being still in his presence.

Is God calling me to this kind of prayer?

Even as I continued to resist the idea but obeyed in practice, God was kind and generous to give me two more very clear invitations to this kind of prayer. In both, he used people whose Christian lives I respected, and who seemed to have a greater gift to discern what the Holy Spirit was saying.

One of my former pastors, Dr. Eloise McDowell, has been a mentor and friend over many years. Prior to pastoring, she was an executive in a large corporation, and I respected her wisdom. As I was facing some difficulties in my work, I asked her to come and pray with me and share some wise counsel. I also sensed she was going to somehow confirm God's invitation to Centering Prayer, but I did not bring up the topic. However, as we sorted through the issues I was facing, out of the blue she asked whether I ever considered just sitting with God in silence. I was surprised at God's confirmation and felt very grateful. This helped me continue the practice, but still my lack of faith persisted a few more years.

There is an element of Centering Prayer that simply requires faith. It requires faith to believe God has called us to it, and it requires faith to believe that he is actively involved in the practice. My questions didn't finally get settled until my second year in the Doctor of Ministry program, when I was anxious about rumors of layoffs in my particular department. I was anxious enough to not be able to trust my discernment. I asked one of my friends to pray for me to help me discern what God wanted me to know about the situation, if anything.

A few days later, he reported that while praying for me, the words, *"God speaks in the silence,"* had come to him, and although he didn't know what that meant, he sensed it was for me. He did not know this, but that week I had been reading a book on Christian mysticism for one of my classes, *The Big Book of Christian Mysticism: The Essential Guide to Contemplative Spirituality,*[114] and the same unusual theme was expressed there: "Contemplation is the prayer of paradox, for in it you relax your mind to listen for a God whose light comes to you as darkness and whose word comes to you as silence."

This was helpful confirmation that God was calling me to this type of prayer. And given all the supporting data from mindfulness research, it seemed a reasonable conclusion that one of the reasons God was calling me to this method was to help manage my anxiety and draw me nearer to him at the same time.

This raises the question of the value of secular mindfulness that does not require any kind of sense of calling. If I as a follower of Christ am not feeling called to Centering Prayer, and yet I'd like to get the benefits of mindfulness, can I still practice it? The answer here is highly individual and worthy of personal discernment, as well as being a good topic to go over with a spiritual director. I would suggest that if the desire is strong enough, perhaps the calling really is there. If unsure, we can always ask God to show the way, and try it for a few weeks and test the fruit.

Cautions

A fascinating study was done in the 1990s by Dr. Margaret M. Paloma, who at the time was a sociology of religion professor at Dayton University in Ohio. She received a grant from Gallup to study the prayer habits of Americans.[115] In particular, she was interested in what types of prayer bring about the most spiritual maturity. She chose the ability to forgive others as a marker for spiritual growth.

She looked at four kinds of prayer to search for this marker: prayer from a book, memorized prayers, conversational prayer, and finally meditative types of prayer similar to the rosary for Catholics or listening prayer for Protestants. The latter is where one spends time in silence waiting to hear from God in the form of an inner impression, an inner symbolic picture, or internal words they feel are from God, while subjecting all of this to all the rules of discernment discussed in Chapter 8. She found the strongest correlation was between meditative prayer and the ability to forgive. People who prayed with this method felt their lives were actively led by God, and they were more able to forgive than those practicing other forms of prayer. This caused me to encourage those I mentored to pursue this type of prayer. The problem was that I was not very discerning as to whether they were ready for it yet. I ended up encouraging people I mentored to follow this path when they were not yet ready, and this unfortunately caused some of them to quit praying.

God's call is essential

I was saddened when my efforts to encourage others to try meditation weren't effective or profitable for them. I think the bottom line is that they either weren't ready for it or God had simply not called them to it in that season of their journey with him.

These instances occurred before I trained as a spiritual director, so I'll use that as an excuse for my ignorance. Then one day I ran across a passage in Richard Foster's book *Prayer, Finding the Heart's True Home,* which lays out quite clearly that contemplative prayer and listening to God in prayer is not for people who are just starting out in personal spiritual practices. He recounts C. S. Lewis's efforts as described by Lewis to his friend Malcolm: "I still think the prayer without words is the best—if one can really achieve it. But I now see that in trying to make it my daily bread I was counting on a greater mental and spiritual strength than I really have. To pray successfully without words, one needs to be 'at the top of one's form.'"[116]

So how do we know when someone is ready for this kind of prayer? This is what Richard Foster says:

> You may want to ask yourself several questions of examination to help evaluate your own readiness:
> "Am I becoming less afraid of being known and owned by God?"
> "Is prayer developing in me as a welcome discipline?"
> "Is it becoming easier for me to receive constructive criticism?"
> "Am I learning to move beyond personal offence and freely forgive those who wronged me?"[117]

Finally, Foster adds that because there is an element of stepping into the supernatural with contemplative prayer, he recommends starting with a simple prayer of protection, such as:

> "By the authority of almighty God, I surround myself with the blood of Christ, and I seal myself with the cross of Christ. All dark and evil spirits must now leave. No influence is allowed to come near to me but that it is first

filtered through the light of Jesus Christ, in whose name
I pray. Amen."[118]

Watch out for discernment quicksand

My final caution involves the process of discerning
whether impressions during meditation are from God or
not. Discernment is spiritually healthy and right. Sometimes, though, an inner impression, especially if it involved the health of a loved one, could trigger anxiety for
me. If the thought I was evaluating was anxiety provoking, it made discernment more difficult. I would feel the
need to seek God more for wisdom and discernment. Once
again, this is good and right, but when it is done to reduce
anxiety, it falls into the category of seeking reassurance,
which, as I described in Chapter 2, only increases anxiety.

Chapter 13

Finding a Greater Love

THERE IS ONE FINAL THOUGHT I would like to leave you with. Finding a measure of healing and freedom from anxiety does not mean we will never be anxious again. Learning how to not engage in avoidance and reassurance seeking when we are anxious is important to defuse the immediate anxiety. Dealing with the root causes can provide long-term relief. Developing a secure attachment to God and meditative prayer can reshape our brains to make them more resilient to anxiety. Yet there is one overarching theme that we need to hang on to for future episodes of anxiety, and that is love.

Love is the ultimate antidote to fear. This is most clearly seen in the discussion on developing a secure attachment to God in Chapter 10. Developing and deepening that secure attachment is a lifelong journey, and so is the awareness of how deeply loved we are by our Creator. As we grow in that sense of secure attachment, we can begin to practice an additional type of prayer in the face of anxiety. We can begin to turn our attention to that love.

One exercise I learned from Fr. Matthew Linn, SJ, is to begin by remembering a time when I felt most loved by a human. When I've chosen that memory, I stay with the feelings it evokes until a sense of joy grows in me. After I have settled into the warmth of that memory, I turn my attention to God. I know that in reality God loves me tremendously more than I felt from that human connection. I can safely then attribute this feeling of being loved to God. Fr. Matt's view is that love is greater than fear, and I hope that as I practice this additional form of prayer, I can find even greater healing in the face of future anxieties.

Knowing cognitively that God loves us is vastly different from an experiential awareness of that love. This is one of two reasons I left this chapter till the end, so that we could first cover a range of ways to connect with God and know his love more experientially. This exercise will be much more effective after we develop that secure attachment to God. Nurturing that experiential awareness of God's love opens new possibilities of resilience in the face of anxiety. When we experience that love, coupled with a cognitive understanding of God's sovereignty, combined with experiences of God exercising that sovereignty and providing for our needs, the feeling of secure attachment has its final fruit. Looking back at the words of Bowlby that I quoted earlier, we could substitute God as the one we are attached to, and the secure base as our time spent in his presence in prayer:

> Throughout adult life the availability of [God as] a responsive attachment figure remains the source of a person's feeling secure. All of us, from the cradle to the grave, are happiest when life is organized as a series of excursions, long or short, from the secure base [of time spent in God's presence in prayer].[119]

The second reason I have left this till the end is that I feel this is a lifelong process for many of us. I know for many this comes easily, and it makes intuitive and cognitive sense to me, but I have so much more to learn in this area. I pray for you, the reader, as well as for those you care for, to know God's love in this way, the way that banishes all fear. I humbly ask for the same prayer for myself.

Appendix A

Rule of Life

This appendix contains some basic ideas and suggestions for helping you create a Personal Rule of Life. Take your time and do it in a reflective space, getting in touch with how God is inviting you along the way in each of the steps below.

Setting the space

Prayer and community are critical in discerning the rhythms we plan to live by. Begin then by praying for the Holy Spirit's leading, that he guide your thoughts and the entire process. It may be a good activity for a retreat day. You may want to spend some time praying about each of the activities below before doing them. Second, enlist the help of some people you trust and get feedback from them. If you don't have a Spiritual Director, consider getting one.

Getting the ingredients ready

The development of a Personal Rule of Life is best done with some helpful inputs. This is by no means a comprehensive list, and you don't have to do all of them, but the more you do, the more helpful it will be.

1. Make a list of your top three spiritual gifts.
2. God often leads us by placing deep desires within us. List the top three desires you have that you are aware of.
3. Make a list of the significant roles in your life, like parent, spouse, son, daughter, engineer, teacher, bus driver, etc.
4. Picture your eighty-fifth birthday. Your family and friends are having a big party for you and they are taking turns offering toasts. Write out five toasts that you want to be given in honor of the life you've lived.
5. Write your own eulogy. What do you want to be said about your life?
6. Write down a list of the one hundred things you want to do in this life. It's OK to repeat things. Keep writing and don't stop to ponder. When you are done, what items have been repeated often?
7. What are your three favorite movies and three favorite books? Do you notice any themes?

Personal mission statement

Write out a mission statement for each of the important roles you've identified in your life now, as well as future roles you envision based on the previous exercises. In addition to the roles, include what you feel God wants for you in caring for your body, your emotional health, and especially your relationship with him. Try to keep the total roles to less than ten or so.

It would look something like this:

1. As a father/mother, I want my kids to know that I have loved them abundantly and unconditionally.

I want them to see my faith lived out and taught to them authentically.

2. As an engineer, I want to give glory to God by continually developing my skills, using them faithfully, and caring about my fellow employees.

3. For my emotional health, I want to have deep friendships that embody vulnerability, trust, and laughter.

4. Etc.

Writing the rule of life

Take the mission statement above and create a list of specific tasks and rhythms that reflect what God is leading you into in each of these areas. Create as many or as few categories as you feel will be helpful. A Rule of Life does not need to be complex. In the table on the facing page are some examples for illustration only.

You can then use the table you made as is, make a graphical version of it, or write it out in sentences that reflect your intentionality in each category.

Living and revisiting

As we live out our Rule, we inevitably need to make adjustments. Some people find it helpful to talk with others about how they are doing with their Personal Rule of Life and to get further input in making changes. It is important that it is not seen as a static and oppressive set of goals.

Additional resources

The Common Rule, by Justin Whitmel Earley
Crafting a Rule of Life, by Stephen Macchia
An Unhurried Leader, by Alan Fadling

CATEGORY	DAILY	WEEKLY	QUARTERLY	ANNUALLY
Parent	Pray for each of my kids daily. Pray with them before bed.	Affirm something in each of my children that is not related to something they achieved. Share with my kids a faith struggle or question I am having. Have at least 4 meals with the kids per week. Play with kids at least 3X a week.	Seek input from someone I trust about my parenting.	Take a weekend to spend with each of the kids separately.
Engineering	Be faithful and give my best with my projects, even when they feel mundane.	Invest in offering significant help to one coworker, whether at work or outside.	Take a class or read up on new developments in the field.	Attend a conference that will help me to broaden my awareness in developments in my field.
Emotional Health	Plan at least an hour of rest a day.	Spend time with one or more close friends 1-2X a week. Be intentionally vulnerable with 2 trusted friends each week.	Plan a larger fun outing with close friends.	Take a vacation with close friends.
Etc.				

Appendix B

For Further Reflection

Chapter 1

- Take a few minutes to ask the Holy Spirit to highlight for you what he most wants you to retain from this book.

Chapter 2

- Ask God to show you what you may be resisting that he wants you to accept. Write down what you think he's saying to you. Ask him for the grace to accept it. Pray the prayer of welcome.

Chapters 3 and 4

- Think about distressing situations in your life where prayer has not helped. Try using the Anxiety Redemption Prayer. Write down how that felt.

Chapter 5

- Ask God to show you if there are areas of social

avoidance or reassurance-seeking in your life he'd like you to start facing. Ask him to show you what next steps he wants you to take. Write down what you think he is saying.

- Write down what you know you've had difficulty accepting about yourself out of pride. Take time to repent and seek forgiveness. You can use the sample prayer in the chapter. If your church tradition emphasizes confession to a priest, make the appointment to do that. Spend time experiencing the freedom and joy that comes with receiving God's forgiveness. Ask for the grace to accept every aspect of who God made you to be on an ongoing basis.

- If you are anxious over too much to do, pray about creating a Personal Rule of Life. Schedule a block of time when you can work through the exercise of creating one provided in Appendix A.

- Ask God to show you if you are anxious because you are pursuing things that are not in his best plans for you. Give him thanks for showing you. Pray for grace to lay down what you are pursuing that is not his desire for you.

Chapter 6

- Ask God to show you how trauma has gotten in the way of your relationship with him and with others. Ask him to show you what, if anything, he wants you to do about that in this season. God has his timing for our healing, and the people he wants us to pray or counsel with. Pray for the next step he wants you to take.

- Try the first step of the Immanuel Approach prayer. Take time to remember a time of feeling close to God. Spend a few minutes recreating the memory. Write down as many of the details as you can remember. Spending at least a few minutes in it helps to conjure up the feelings. Ask Jesus where he is in the scene. Don't try to imagine him. Just relax and see what he shows you. Once you have a sense of that, enjoy being with him in that memory for a while.
- Try the exercise of receiving attunement from God as outlined at the end of the chapter.

Chapter 7

- Take the time to bring to God how you feel about what is difficult in your life. Make sure you tell him as much about your feelings as possible.
- Ask God how he wants you to integrate this exercise into your regular prayer practice.

Chapter 8

- Try to integrate the prayer of examen into your daily prayer for a week or two. Do you notice any change in how you think or feel about your spiritual life?

Chapter 9

- Ask God to show you what he is inviting you to in prayer. If that feels more than you can do comfortably, pray for the grace to pray five minutes more than you are currently praying. Then add those five minutes. After that begins to feel life-giving, ask for grace to pray five minutes more, and so on, until you reach the goal you feel you heard from God.

Chapter 10

- Write down what it means for you personally to trust God. Be as detailed as you can. Take time to pray for how God wants you to grow in that trust.

Chapter 11

- Practice Lectio Divina as outlined in the chapter on Psalm 121. Write down what God has done in your heart as you did it.
- Take time for a walk in nature. Ask the Holy Spirit to speak to you. Write down any impressions you think might be coming from him. Write down what they stir in you in response.
- Ask the Holy Spirit to guide your thoughts to specific times God's providence has been at work in your life. Journal through each event, take time to give thanks. Note how you feel after this exercise.

Chapter 12

- Ask God if he'd have you try Centering Prayer. If you sense the invitation, pray a prayer of protection and then try it for twenty minutes twice a day as suggested in the chapter. After a week or two, what do you notice is shifting for you?

Chapter 13

- Try the exercise described in the chapter, to remember an episode of experiencing loving or being loved, and then shifting your attention to God, knowing how much greater his love is than that memory. Ask God for experiences of his love that drives away all fear.

Endnotes

1. Richard Foster, *Streams of Living Water* (New York: Harper-Collins Publishers, 1998), 58, 96, 133, 182, 233, 272.

2. Individual studies cited here help to support and provide insight, but they are not intended to communicate established understanding of the scientific community on a given topic, which may not come until many more studies replicate the findings.

3. Stephen P. Stratton, "Mindfulness and Contemplation: Secular and Religious Traditions in Western Context," *Counseling and Values* 60, no. 1 (2015): 100-118.

4. Jon Kabat-Zinn, *Wherever You Go, There You Are: Mindfulness Meditation in Everyday Life* (New York: Hachette Books, 1994), 4.

5. Gregg Blanton, *Contemplation and Counseling: An Integrative Model for Practitioners* (Downers Grove, IL: InterVarsity Press, 2019), 4.

6. Margaret Wehrenberg and Steven M. Prinz, *The Anxious Brain* (New York and London: W.W. Norton & Company, 2007), 155.

7. Kenneth E. Bailey, *Jesus Through Middle Eastern Eyes: Cultural Studies in the Gospels* (Downers Grove, IL: InterVarsity Press Academic, 2008), 324.

8. Steven C. Hayes, Kirk D. Strosahl, and Kelly G. Wilson, *Acceptance and Commitment Therapy: The Process and Practice of Mindful Change* (New York, NY: The Guilford Process, 2016), 270.

9. Hayes, Strosahl, and Wilson, *Acceptance and Commitment Therapy*, 273-275.

10. Steven C. Hayes et al., "Acceptance and Commitment Therapy: Model, process and outcomes," *Behavior Research and Therapy* 44, no. 1 (2006): 1-25.

11. Adele Calhoun, *Spiritual Disciplines Handbook: Practices That Transform Us* (Downers Grove, IL: IVP, 2015), 288.

12. Robert A. Emmons and Charles M. Shelton, "Gratitude and the Science of Positive Psychology," in *The Handbook of Positive Psychology*, ed. C. R. Snyder and Shane J. Lopez (New York: Oxford University Press, 2002), 460.

13. R. A. Emmons and M. E. McCullough, "Counting Blessings Versus Burdens: An Experimental Investigation of Gratitude and Subjective Well-being in Daily Life," *Journal of Personality and Social Psychology* 84, no. 2 (2003): 377-389. https://doi.org/10.1037//0022-3514.84.2.377

14. R. W. Lau and S. T. Cheng, "Gratitude Lessens Death Anxiety," *European Journal of Ageing* 8, no. 3 (2011): 169.

15. Glenn R. Fox et al., "Neural Correlates of Gratitude," *Frontiers in Psychology* 6 (2015), article 1491.

16. Karl Lehman, *Outsmarting Yourself* (Las Vegas: This Joy Books, 2011), 178-179.

17. Viktor Frankl, *Man's Search for Meaning* (Boston: Beacon Press, 2006), 97.

18. Louis Cozolino, *The Neuroscience of Human Relationships* (New York and London: W.W. Norton & Company, 2014, 2006), 298.

19. Cozolino, *Neuroscience of Human Relationships*, 302.

20. Lydia Fehm, Katja Beesdo, Frank Jacobi, and Agnes Fiedler, "Social anxiety disorder above and below the diagnostic threshold: Prevalence, comorbidity and impairment in the general population," *Social Psychiatry and Psychiatric Epidemiology* 43, no. 4 (2008): 257-265.

21. Cozolino, *Neuroscience of Human Relationships*, 304.

22. Anca Dobrean and Costina-Ruxandra Pasarelu, *Impact of Social Media on Social Anxiety: A Systematic Review, New Developments in Anxiety Disorders* (Croatia: IntechOpen, 2016).

23. Onder Baltaci, "The Predictive Relationships between the Social Media Addiction and Social Anxiety, Loneliness, and Happiness," *International Journal of Progressive Education* 15, no. 4 (2019): p.73.

24. Graham Davey, "Is There an Anxiety Epidemic?," *Psychology Today*, last modified November 6, 2018, https://www.psychologytoday.com/us/blog/why-we-worry/201811/is-there-anxiety-epidemic

25. Margaret Wehrenberg and Steven M. Prinz, *The Anxious Brain* (New York and London: W.W. Norton & Company, 2007), 198-199.

26. Philip Yancey, *The Jesus I Never Knew* (Grand Rapids,

MI: Zondervan, 1995), 117-118.

27. "About Us," *Immanuel Approach*, WordPress, accessed November 10, 2020, https://www.immanuelapproach.com/about-us/.

28. Karl D. Lehman, *The Immanuel Approach for Emotional Healing and for Life* (Evanston, IL: Immanuel Publishing, 2016).

29. Lehman, *Immanuel Approach*, 709.

30. Karl Lehman, *Outsmarting Yourself* (Libertyville: This Joy! Books, 2011), 14.

31. Lehman, *Outsmarting Yourself*, 21.

32. Lehman, *Outsmarting Yourself*, 102.

33. E. James Wilder, Anna Kang, John Loppnow, and Sungshim Loppnow, *Joyful Journey: Listening to Immanuel* (East Peoria, IL: Shepherd's House Inc., 2015), 28.

34. Lehman, *Outsmarting Yourself*, 156.

35. Lehman, *Outsmarting Yourself*, 181.

36. Lehman, *Outsmarting Yourself*, 178.

37. Lehman, *Outsmarting Yourself*, 194.

38. Lehman, *Immanuel Approach*, 586.

39. Elisha Albright Hoffman, "I Must Tell Jesus All of My Troubles," 1894.

40. Wilder, Kang, Loppnow, and Loppnow, *Joyful Journey*, 20.

41. These steps are a paraphrased summary of the Immanuel Approach as it can be used in personal prayer. For a much fuller explanation with extensive examples and resources, go to http://www.immanuelapproach.com.

42. Karl D. Lehman, *The Immanuel Approach for Emotional Healing and for Life* (Evanston, IL: Immanuel Publishing, 2016), 7.

43. Wilder, Kang, Loppnow, and Loppnow, *Joyful Journey*, 49.

44. Scot McKnight, *Praying with the Church: Following Jesus Daily, Hourly, Today* (Cape Cod, MA: Paraclete Press, 2006), chapter 5.

45. McKnight, *Praying with the Church*, location 746 of 2198.

46. Curt Thompson, *Anatomy of the Soul* (Carol Stream, IL: Tyndale House Publishers, 2010), 150.

47. Thompson, *Anatomy of the Soul*, 3-4.

48. Walter Brueggemann, *Spirituality of the Psalms* (Minneapolis, MN: Fortress Press, 2001), 290-291.

49. Brueggemann, *Spirituality of the Psalms*, 379-383.

50. Thompson, *Anatomy of the Soul*, 151-152.

51. Richard G. Tedeschi and Lawrence G. Calhoun, "Posttraumatic growth: Conceptual foundations and empirical evidence,"

Psychological Inquiry 15, no. 1 (2004): 1-18.

52. E. James Wilder, Anna Kang, John Loppnow, and Sungshim Loppnow, Joyful Journey: *Listening to Immanuel* (East Peoria, IL: Shepherd's House Inc., 2015), 27.

53. J. I. Harris et al., "Coping functions of prayer and posttraumatic growth," *International Journal for the Psychology of Religion* 20, no. 1 (2010).

54. James Martin, *The Jesuit Guide to (Almost) Everything: A Spirituality for Real Life* (New York: HarperOne, 2012), 311.

55. Evan Howard, *The Brazos Introduction to Christian Spirituality* (Grand Rapids, MI: Brazos Press, 2008), location 385 of 1517.

56. Briege McKenna and Henry Libersat, *Miracles Do Happen* (Ann Arbor, MI: Servant Publications, 1987), 25-26.

57. Henri Nouwen, *Discernment: Reading the Signs of Daily Life* (New York: HarperOne, 2013), location 332 of 3532.

58. David Benner, *Desiring God's Will: Aligning Our Hearts with the Heart of God* (Downers Grove, IL: InterVarsity Press, 2005), 14-15.

59. Martin, *Jesuit Guide*, 312.

60. Martin, *Jesuit Guide*, 306-307.

61. Martin, *Jesuit Guide* 316.

62. Martin, *Jesuit Guide*, 308.

63. Martin, *Jesuit Guide*, 316.

64. Martin, *Jesuit Guide*, 309.

65. Martin, *Jesuit Guide*, 317.

66. Martin, *Jesuit Guide*, 318-319.

67. Martin, *Jesuit Guide*, 323-25.

68. Martin, *Jesuit Guide*, 103.

69. Martin, *Jesuit Guide*, 143.

70. John White, *The Fight* (Downers Grove, IL: InterVarsity Press, 1976), 21-22.

71. Curt Thompson, *Anatomy of the Soul* (Carol Stream, IL: Tyndale House Publishers, 2010), 79.

72. Thompson, *Anatomy of the Soul*, 66.

73. Jerry Bridges, *Trusting God* (Carol Stream, IL: NavPress, 1988).

74. Peter Kreeft, *Making Sense Out of Suffering* (Cincinnati: Franciscan Press, 1986).

75. Brian McLaren, *A New Kind of Christian: A Tale of Two Friends on a Spiritual Journey* (Philadelphia: Fortress Press, 2019).

76. Louis Cozolino, *The Neuroscience of Human Relationships*

(New York and London: W.W. Norton & Company, 2014, 2006), 145.

77. Cozolino, *Neuroscience of Human Relationships,* 151.

78. John Bowlby, *A Secure Base: Parent-Child Attachment and Healthy Human Development* (London and USA: Basic Books 1988), 45-46.

79. Bowlby, *Secure Base,* 11.

80. Andrew Newberg and Mark R. Waldman, *How God Changes Your Brain* (New York: Ballantine Books, 2010), 48.

81. Bowlby, *Secure Base,* 62.

82. Curt Thompson, *Anatomy of the Soul* (Carol Stream, IL: Tyndale House Publishers, 2010), 118.

83. Thompson, *Anatomy of the Soul,* 133.

84. Thompson, *Anatomy of the Soul,* 41.

85. Michael W. Vasey and Mark R. Dadds, eds., *The Developmental Psychopathology of Anxiety* (Oxford University Press, 2001), 278-303, Created from hope on 2020-09-03 18:27:34.

86. Margaret Wehrenberg and Steven M. Prinz, *The Anxious Brain* (New York and London: W.W. Norton & Company, 2007), 4.

87. Wehrenberg and Prinz, *Anxious Brain,* 26.

88. Wehrenberg and Prinz, *Anxious Brain,* 26.

89. Louis Cozolino, *The Neuroscience of Human Relationships* (New York and London: W.W. Norton & Company, 2014, 2006), 310-311.

90. Wehrenberg and Prinz, *Anxious Brain,* 28.

91. Bessel A. Van Der Kolk, Jennifer A. Burbridge, and Joji Suzuki, "The Psychobiology of Traumatic Memory: Clinical Implications of Neuroimaging Studies," *Annals of the New York Academy of Sciences,* December 17, 2006, 99-113.

92. Michael D. De Bellis et al., "Brain Structures in Pediatric Maltreatment-Related Posttraumatic Stress Disorder: A Sociodemographically Matched Study," *Biological Psychiatry* 52, no. 11 (2002).

93. J. Douglas Bremner, Lawrence H. Staib, Danny Kaloupek, Steven M. Southwick, Robert Soufer, and Dennis S. Charney, "Neural Correlates of Exposure to Traumatic Pictures and Sound in Vietnam Combat Veterans with and without Posttraumatic Stress Disorder: A Positron Emission Tomography Study," *Biological Psychiatry* 45, no. 7 (1999): 806-816.

94. Uri Bergman, "Speculations on the Neurobiology of EMDR," presented at Harvard University-Cambridge Hospital symposium on EMDR, moderated by Judith Lewis Herman,

M.D., October 18, 1996.

95. Joshua L. Roffman, Carl D. Marci, Debra M. Glick, and Darin D. Dougherty, "Neuroimaging and the Functional Neuroanatomy of Psychotherapy," *Psychological Medicine* 35, no. 10 (2005): 1385-1398.

96. Andrew Newberg and Mark R. Waldman, *How God Changes Your Brain* (New York: Ballantine Books, 2010), 17.

97. Thompson, *Anatomy of the Soul*, 160.

98. Jon Kabat-Zinn, *Wherever You Go, There You Are: Mindfulness Meditation in Everyday Life*, 10th ed. (New York, NY: Hyperion, 2005), 145-146.

99. Joshua L. Roffman, Carl D. Marci, Debra M. Glick, and Darin D. Dougherty, "Neuroimaging and the Functional Neuroanatomy of Psychotherapy," *Psychological Medicine* 35, no. 10 (2005): 1385-1398.

100. Amy B. Wachholtz and Kenneth I. Pargament, "Is spirituality a critical ingredient of meditation? Comparing the effects of spiritual meditation, secular meditation, and relaxation on spiritual, psychological, cardiac, and pain outcomes," *Journal of Behavioral Medicine* 28, no. 4 (2005): 383.

101. Andrew Newberg et al., "Cerebral blood flow during meditative prayer: preliminary findings and methodological issues," *Perceptual and Motor Skills* 97, no. 2 (2003): 625-630.

102. Newberg and Waldman, *How God Changes Your Brain*, 48.

103. Eugene H. Peterson, *The Contemplative Pastor: Returning to the Art of Spiritual Direction* (Grand Rapids, MI: Eerdmans Publishing Company, 1989), 105.

104. Newberg and Waldman, *How God Changes Your Brain*, 62.

105. Thompson, *Anatomy of the Soul*, 178.

106. James Martin, *The Jesuit Guide to (Almost) Everything: A Spirituality for Real Life* (New York: HarperOne, 2012), 18.

107. Adele Calhoun, *Spiritual Disciplines Handbook: Practices That Transform Us* (Downers Grove, IL: InterVarsity Press, 2015), 188-189.

108. This model is adapted from the website diningwithgod.org.

109. M. Robert Mulholland Jr., *Shaped by the Word: The Power of Scripture in Spiritual Formation*, rev. ed. (Nashville, TN: Upper Room Books, 2001).

110. Thompson, *Anatomy of the Soul*, 177.

111. Eugene Peterson, *A Long Obedience in the Same Direction: Discipleship in an Instant Society* (Downers Grove, IL: InterVarsity Press, 2000), 64.

112. Thomas H. Green, *When the Well Runs Dry: Prayer Beyond the Beginnings* (Notre Dame, IN: Ave Maria Press, 2007), 152.

113. Eugene H. Peterson, *The Contemplative Pastor* (Grand Rapids, MI; Eerdmans, 1993), 103-104.

114. Carl McColman, *The Big Book of Christian Mysticism: The Essential Guide to Contemplative Spirituality* (Charlottesville, VA: Hampton Roads, 2010), 213.

115. Margaret Paloma and George Gallup, *Varieties of Prayer: A Survey Report* (Philadelphia, PA: Trinity Press International), 1991.

116. Richard J. Foster, *Prayer: Finding the Heart's True Home* (San Francisco, CA: HarperSanFrancisco, 1992), 156.

117. Foster, *Prayer*, 157.

118. Foster, *Prayer*, 157.

119. John Bowlby, *A Secure Base: Parent-Child Attachment and Healthy Human Development* (London and USA: Basic Books, 1988), 62.

REFERENCES

Bailey, Kenneth E. *Jesus Through Middle Eastern Eyes: Cultural Studies in the Gospels.* Downers Grove, IL: InterVarsity Press Academic, 2008.

Benner, David. *Desiring God's Will: Aligning Our Hearts with the Heart of God.* Downers Grove, IL: InterVarsity Press, 2005.

Bergman, Uri. "Speculations on the Neurobiology of EMDR." Presented at Harvard University-Cambridge Hospital, at an all-day symposium on EMDR. Moderated by Judith Lewis Herman, M.D. October 18, 1996.

Blanton, Gregg. *Contemplation and Counseling: An Integrative Model for Practitioners.* Downers Grove, IL: InterVarsity Press, 2019.

Bowlby, .John *A Secure Base: Parent-Child Attachment and Healthy Human Development.* London and USA: Basic Books 1988.

Bremner, J. Douglas, Lawrence H. Staib, Danny Kaloupek, Steven M. Southwick, Robert Soufer, and Dennis S. Charney. "Neural Correlates of Exposure to Traumatic Pictures and Sound in Vietnam Combat Veterans with and without Posttraumatic Stress Disorder: A Positron Emission Tomography Study." *Biological Psychiatry* 45, no. 7 (1999): 806-816.

Bridges, Jerry. *Trusting God.* Carol Stream, IL: NavPress in alliance with Tyndale House, 1988.

Brueggemann, Walter. *Spirituality of the Psalms.* Minneapolis, MN: Fortress Press, 2002.

Calhoun, Adele. *Spiritual Disciplines Handbook: Practices That Transform Us.* Downers Grove, IL: InterVarsity Press, 2015.

Cameron, Julia. *The Artist's Way: A Spiritual Path to Higher Creativity.* New York: Penguin, 2002.

Cloud, Henry. *9 Things You Simply Must Do to Succeed in Love and Life.* Nashville, TN: Thomas Nelson Publishers, 2007.

Cozolino, Louis. *The Neuroscience of Human Relationships.* New York and London: W.W. Norton & Company, 2014, 2006,

Davey, Graham. "Is There an Anxiety Epidemic?" *Psychology Today.* Last modified November 6, 2018. https://www.psychologytoday.com/us/blog/why-we-worry/201811/is-there-anxiety-epidemic

De Bellis, Michael D., Matcheri S. Keshavan, Heather Shifflett, Satish Iyengar, Sue R. Beers, Julie Hall, and Grace Moritz. "Brain Structures in Pediatric Maltreatment-Related Posttraumatic Stress Disorder: A Sociodemographically Matched Study." *Biological Psychiatry* 52, no. 11 (2002).

Emmons, Robert A., and Charles M. Shelton. "Gratitude and the Science of Positive Psychology." In *The Handbook of Positive Psychology,,*edited by C. R. Snyder and Shane J. Lopez. New York: Oxford University Press, 2002.

Emmons, R. A., and M. E. McCullough. "Counting blessings versus burdens: an experimental investigation of gratitude and subjective well-being in daily life." *Journal of personality and social psychology* 84, no. 2 (2003): 377-389. https://doi.org/10.1037//0022-3514.84.2.377

Foster, Richard. *Prayer: Finding the Heart's True Home.* San Francisco, CA: HarperSanFrancisco, 1992.

Foster, Richard. *Streams of Living Water.* New York: Harper-Collins Publishers, 1998.

Fox, Glenn R., Jonas Caplan, Hanna Damasio, and Antonio Damasio. "Neural Correlates of Gratitude." *Frontiers in Psychology* 6 (2015).

Fox, Jesse, Daniel Gutierrez, Jessica Haas, Dinesh Braganza, and Christine Berger. "A Phenomenological Investigation of Centering Prayer Using Conventional Content Analysis." *Pastoral Psychology* 64, no. 6 (2015): 803–825. https://doi.org/10.1007/s11089-015-0657-1

Frankl, Viktor E. *Man's Search for Meaning.* Boston, MA: Beacon Press, 2014.Green, Thomas H. *When the Well Runs Dry: Prayer Beyond the Beginnings.* Notre Dame, IN: Ave Maria Press, 2007.

Harris, J. I., Christopher R. Erbes, Brian E. Engdahl, Richard G. Tedeschi, Raymond H. Olson, Ann Marie M. Winskowski, and Joelle McMahill. "Coping functions of prayer and posttraumatic growth." *International Journal for the Psychology of Religion* 20, no. 1 (2010): 26-38, doi: 10.1080/10508610903418103.

Hayes, Steven C., Jason B. Luoma, Frank W. Bond, Akihiko Masuda, and Jason Lillis. "Acceptance and Commitment Therapy: Model, process and outcomes." *Behavior Research and Therapy* 44, no. 1 (2006): 1-25.

Hayes, Steven C., Kirk D. Strosahl, and Kelly G. Wilson. *Acceptance and Commitment Therapy: The*

Process and Practice of Mindful Change. New York, NY: The Guilford Process, 2016.

Hoffman, Elisha A. 1893. "I Must Tell Jesus All of My Troubles."

Howard, Evan B. *The Brazos Introduction to Christian Spirituality.* Grand Rapids, MI: Brazos Press, 2008.

Kabat-Zinn, Jon. *Wherever You Go, There You Are: Mindfulness Meditation in Everyday Life.* 10th ed. New York, NY: Hyperion, 2005.

Kreeft, Peter. *Making Sense Out of Suffering.* Cincinnati: Franciscan Press, 1986.

Lau, R. W. and Sheung-Tak Cheng. "Gratitude Lessens Death Anxiety." *European Journal of Ageing* 8, no. 3 (2011).

Lehman, Karl. *The Immanuel Approach for Emotional Healing and for Life.* Evanston, IL: Immanuel Publishing, 2016.

Lehman, Karl. "Jesus Is Bigger Than All the Badness in the World." Immanuel Approach video, 33:08. May 13, 2020, https://www.youtube.com/watch?v=kOpC5gvgCSY

Lehman, Karl. *Outsmarting Yourself.* Las Vegas: This Joy Books, 2011.

Martin, James. *The Jesuit Guide to (Almost) Everything: A Spirituality for Real Life.* New York: HarperOne, 2012.

McColman, Carl. *The Big Book of Christian Mysticism: The Essential Guide to Contemplative Spirituality.* Charlottesville, VA: Hampton Roads, 2010. Kindle eBook.

McKenna, Briege, and Henry Libersat. *Miracles Do Happen.* Ann Arbor, MI: Servant Publications, 1987.

McKnight, Scot. *Praying with the Church: Following*

Jesus Daily, Hourly, Today. Brewster, MA: Paraclete Press, 2006. Kindle ebook.

McLaren, Brian. *A New Kind of Christian: A Tale of Two Friends on a Spiritual Journey*. Philadelphia: Fortress Press, 2019.

Miranda, Talita, Silvia Caldeira, Harley de Oliveria, Denise Hollanda /Lunes, Denismar Nogueira, Erika Chaves, and Emilia de Carvalho. "Intercessory Prayer on Spiritual Distress, Spiritual Coping, Anxiety, Depression and Salivary Amylase in Breast Cancer Patients During Radiotherapy: Randomized Clinical Trial." *Journal of Religion and Health* 59, no. 1 (2020): 365-380, doi: 10.1007/s10943-019-00827-5.

Mulholland, Robert, Jr. *Shaped by the Word: The Power of Scripture in Spiritual Formation*. Revised Edition. Nashville, TN: Upper Room Books, 2001.

Newberg, Andrew, and Mark R. Waldman. *How God Changes Your Brain*. New York: Ballantine Books, 2010.

Newberg, Andrew, Michael Pourdehnad, Abass Alavi, and Eugene G. d'Aquili. "Cerebral blood flow during meditative prayer: Preliminary findings and methodological issues." *Perceptual and Motor Skills* 97, no. 2 (2003): 625–30.

Nouwen, Henri J. M. *Discernment: Reading the Signs of Daily Life*. New York: HarperOne, 2013. Kindle ebook.

Paloma, Margaret M., and George H. Gallup. *Varieties of Prayer: A Survey Report*. Philadelphia, PA: Trinity Int., 1991.

Passing the Peace After a Crisis. Version 3.1. East Peoria, IL: Shepherd's House Inc., 2015.

Peterson, Eugene. *The Contemplative Pastor: Returning to the Art of Spiritual Direction.* Grand Rapids, MI: Eerdmans Publishing Company, 1989.

Peterson, Eugene. *A Long Obedience in the Same Direction: Discipleship in an Instant Society.* Downers Grove, IL: InterVarsity Press, 2000.

Roffman, Joshua L., Carl D. Marci, Debra M. Glick, and Darin D. Dougherty. "Neuroimaging and the functional neuroanatomy of psychotherapy." *Psychological Medicine* 35, no. 10 (2005): 1385-1398.

Stratton, Stephen P. "Mindfulness and Contemplation: Secular and Religious Traditions in Western Context." *Counseling and Values* 60, no. 1 (2015): 100-118.

Tedeschi, Richard G., and Lawrence G. Calhoun. "Posttraumatic growth: Conceptual foundations and empirical evidence." *Psychological Inquiry* 15, no. 1 (2004): 1-18.

Thompson, Curt. *Anatomy of the Soul.* Carol Stream, IL: Tyndale House Publishers, 2010.

Vasey, Michael W., and Mark R. Dadds, eds. *The Developmental Psychopathology of Anxiety.* Oxford University Press, 2001. ProQuest Ebook Central. http://ebookcentral.proquest.com/lib/hope/detail.action?docID=272877.

Wachholtz, A., and Kenneth Pargament. "Is spirituality a critical ingredient of meditation? Comparing the effects of spiritual meditation, secular meditation, and relaxation on spiritual, psychological, cardiac, and pain outcomes." *Journal of Behavioral Medicine* 28, no. 4 (2005): 369–384.

Wehrenberg, Margaret, and Steven M. Prinz. *The Anxious Brain: The Neurobiological Basis of Anxiety*

Disorders and How to Effectively Treat Them. New York and London: W.W. Norton & Company, 2007.

White, John. *The Fight: A Practical Handbook of Christian Living.* Downers Grove, IL: InterVarsity Press, 1976.

Wilder, E. James, Anna Kang, John Loppnow, and Sungshim Loppnow. *Joyful Journey: Listening to Immanuel.* East Peoria, IL: Shepherd's House Inc., 2015.

Yancey, Philip. *The Jesus I Never Knew.* Grand Rapids, MI: Zondervan Publishing House, 1995.